# GHOS

## *AND*

# EERIE LEGENDS

## *OF*

# CHESTER COUNTY,

## PENNSYLVANIA

Kevin Lagowski

SCHIFFER
PUBLISHING

4880 Lower Valley Road • Atglen, PA 19310

Edited by Ian Robertson
Designed by Jack Chappell
Cover design by Jack Chappell
Type set in Caslon/Scotch Display/Baskerville

ISBN: 978-0-7643-6911-7
ePub: 978-1-5073-0551-5
Printed in China

Published by Schiffer Publishing, Ltd.
4880 Lower Valley Road
Atglen, PA 19310
Phone: (610) 593-1777; Fax: (610) 593-2002
Email: info@schifferbooks.com
Web: www.schifferbooks.com

For our complete selection of fine books on this and related subjects, please visit our website at www.schifferbooks.com. You may also write for a free catalog.

Schiffer Publishing's titles are available at special discounts for bulk purchases for sales promotions or premiums. Special editions, including personalized covers, corporate imprints, and excerpts, can be created in large quantities for special needs. For more information, contact the publisher.

*Death cannot kill what never dies.*
—William Penn, 1682

*Hollywood to me is a place to work. Home is Chester County.*
—Claude Rains, 1950

*I ain't afraid of no ghosts.*
—Ray Parker Jr., 1984

# CONTENTS

# Introduction

Ah, beautiful Chester County, Pennsylvania. The rolling hills, the quaint towns, that connection to nature and history that feels quintessentially American. It is about as old as the "New World" gets—a true slice of American pie, which I suppose is appropriate, given that the county's southeastern border is literally formed by a "wedge" that butts up against it. Over the past few decades, Chester County has served to inspire and act as a backdrop for the art of Andrew Wyeth, the music of Jim Croce, and the films of M. Night Shyamalan. But of course, the legacy of Chester County goes much further back than the lifetime of anyone still living today.

Speaking of its borders, Chester County was much larger when it was founded in 1682 and was created as one of Pennsylvania's three original counties. Decades later its western portion was lopped off to create Lancaster County, and then it received a trim up north when Berks County was formed from the surrounding area. Finally, in 1789, Delaware County was made from the eastern portion of Chester County, and "Delco" was officially born.

We are now left with a county that ranks just twenty-eighth in total area (although seventh in population) among Pennsylvania's sixty-seven counties. It is bordered by Lancaster County to the west, largely by the Octoraro Creek and its tributaries. To the northwest is a rather unexciting, straight-line boundary with Berks County. It meets up with its neighbor to the northeast, Montgomery County, at the banks of the Schuylkill (insert Philly accent here). To the east, the Brandywine River/Creek forms a small portion of its boundary with Delaware County, which makes geographical sense. But the rest of the county line is as confusing as can be, a weird zigzagging dance through neighborhoods and fields that probably made sense once upon a time, but I didn't feel like researching because:

(a) It is not the point of this book, and
(b) even if I did get an answer, it would probably be boring.

Finally, you have that pesky "wedge" and the infamous "arc" border with the state of Delaware at the southeastern corner of Chester County, and then the famed Mason-Dixon Line slashing from east to west separating Chester County and the entire state of Pennsylvania from the "Deep South" of Maryland. At this point I have proven that I can look at a map and write words about it, but let this all serve to set the stage and establish a backdrop for these tales of folklore, ghosts, and the like.

The culture and history here in Chester County (and I say "here" because I sit within its borders as I write this) are points of pride for locals. Other regions lay claim to similar feelings, but there is just something unique about the juxtaposition of Chester County's largely pastoral landscape with a partially urban identity due to the county's proximity to population centers such as Philadelphia and Wilmington.

Let me also assure you that when I say Chester County, I do actually mean Chester County. For this book we will be staying within the county limits, with a few exceptions where we have to traipse just across the line because some places, such as Valley Forge, are so sprawling that they span two counties. This narrow focus is somewhat restrictive, but we might as well just play by the arbitrary rules that we have established for ourselves. Rules are fun like that.

Also, regarding the tone of this book, while I personally enjoy horror and being generally creeped out, it would be too much of a challenge to keep that kind of facade up for an entire book. So what you will get is this: an honest portrait of these tales and legends that is eerie and unsettling when necessary, but also a healthy dose of skepticism for those stores that are generic or hokey enough to deserve it, in my opinion. I will also attempt to paint an accurate historical picture of these tales and put things into proper context while introducing a vein of humor, sometimes dark humor, in many places throughout these bite-size stories of Chester County.

The goal is to come away with a greater appreciation and knowledge of the area, some interesting stories, and, I hope, the desire to check out some of the places mentioned. Some of the topics herein could (and have) inspired entire books, so I am going for the heart of the matter and leaving room for anyone to explore further on their own if they desire. While I would love to be more comprehensive on a lot of these subjects, that would simply stray too far from what this book is supposed to be about. The end result here is not a book that is simply chock-full of paranormal encounters—I have read through a number of these and I'm frankly not much of a fan. Instead, this is meant to be part local history and part travelogue, with a dash of the mysterious thrown in when applicable. Simply telling a story of an average person seeing an apparition at their private residence in Chester County is not good enough; the places and the stories should matter to the general public.

I have sorted the topics into chapters by places (graveyards, taverns, etc.), which is a convenient way to separate the tales told within. And I have even included GPS coordinates for each of the sites, although some will be more accurate than others, owing to how large or how specific the locales are. After all, ghosts and legends can't always be contained in one specific place. I'll also use the phrase "As of this writing . . ." or something similar at various times throughout this book, so fair warning. The landscape is always changing, so if I reference a particular business as being currently at a site and it is gone by the time you read this, don't shoot the messenger.

At any rate, perhaps all of this will encourage you to explore and take in some of these areas of interest. That is if it is legal to do so, since not all the places mentioned herein can be trod without special permission. Just use your common sense. If not, an otherworldly being may just drop by to kindly (or not so kindly) steer you in a different direction.

We are fortunate to live in a place so steeped in history, albeit in a part of the world that practically still has new-car smell when you compare it to some of the other locations around the globe where you can visit sites that are thousands of years old. Still, there is a lot here to visit and enjoy, with many sites hiding a history that might not be readily apparent. The people of Chester County, past (sometimes very past) and present, have a wonderful tradition of writing about and passing down tales of the notable personalities and events that have transpired here over the decades and centuries, which sometimes persist in the form of folklore and the supernatural.

These are their stories.

# ONE

Ghosts and Legends
in the Graveyard

It is not a difficult concept. If you want to talk about ghosts, spooks, specters, or whatever might go bump in the night, the first place you start looking is in a cemetery. Chester County isn't unique in this regard, of course, since virtually any graveyard in the United States and beyond has a tale or two associated with it—creepy statues that come to life at midnight, apparitions wandering among the tombstones, and the like. The collective imagination tends to run wild when one ponders the eerie stillness and the exclusively dead company that a cemetery offers, after all.

Still, this area does have its own unique feel, with history and geography coming together to make for some interesting cases throughout Chester County. Sometimes the cemetery in question is just the endpoint of a curious tale; in other cases there might be something unique about the burying ground itself that adds to the legend in a tangible way. Or maybe a resident of that particular cemetery had a noteworthy life or death (or both). No matter the case, these places connect us to the past, simultaneously preserving history while also showing its steady decay. Time waits for no man, while its passage allows tales to be told, twisted, retold, and perhaps rediscovered and interpreted anew.

I am one of those "cemetery ghoul" types myself, having started a running tally of famous graves that I have visited over the years. My feeling is that, especially if you never met the person, this is the closest that you will get to rubbing elbows with them. How else was I ever going to get near Mark Twain, Robert Frost, or Rod Serling? We might as well take advantage of what we can. The idea of closeness to a deceased individual is something that humans subscribe to; why even visit the grave of a loved one to begin with if there wasn't some meaning attached to it? Let's just visit while we can—before the script is flipped on us.

While I submit that any graveyard is a place worthy of interest, thanks to the lives led by those who permanently reside there, here are a select few burial places from around Chester County that stand out for the stories and enduring mysteries that lie within their walls and below their grounds.

# The Ticking Tomb

Location: London Tract Church Cemetery
400 Sharpless Road, Landenberg
39.74649, −75.77500

A requisite creepy old cemetery, the Mason-Dixon Line, and possibly Edgar Allan Poe are all wrapped up in the story of the Ticking Tomb. There's really something for everybody.

We will head all the way back to 1764, when surveyors Charles Mason and Jeremiah Dixon (both of whom were also astronomers) were assigned to undertake the large task of defining and marking the boundaries that separated the colonies of Pennsylvania and Maryland. This work also included surveying the western and southern borders of Delaware, since the future state was simply the "lower counties" of Pennsylvania at the time.

Using all kinds of fancy equipment and measurements to figure things out, Mason and Dixon started in Philadelphia and went south, then worked westward. As they were in the Landenberg area of Chester County, the seminal event that lends itself to the mystery of the Ticking Tomb occurred. Or maybe it didn't really happen; who is to say?

Still, the story goes that a young child crawled or otherwise stumbled into the surveyors' camp. There, in Mason's tent, he began to cry and, depending on whom you ask, either Mason or one of his assistants grabbed his chronometer (pocket watch), figuring that the ticking gadget would soothe the child in some way, because kids are dumb like that. Then the child ate it.

Never mind the fact that the story relies on the supposition that an adult man was surprised or overpowered enough to let a small child grab and then ingest a piece of machinery, since it is also worth wondering just how a child (sometimes reported as being a baby) would be both old enough to be able to make its way out of the woods and into a camp on its own yet still have the "little kid instincts" to eat a watch. It probably helps if you don't think too hard about it.

At any rate, the child's name was discovered to be Fithian Minuit once he was brought into town and supposedly returned to his extremely inattentive parents. But poor Fithian still had the gizmo inside him, ticking away. In one version of the story, Mason was so incensed at the loss of his valuable instrument that he cursed the little boy to a lifetime without peace, thanks to the constant ticking of the watch inside him. Seems pretty harsh on Mason's part, and it also makes you wonder about the rules governing curses. Can any old person put them on someone else, and for something as low level as eating their watch? The kid did not seem to deserve all that much.

Still, it appears that Fithian Minuit made out okay for the rest of his life on Earth, even after ingesting a piece of metal and then possibly being cursed by Charles Mason.

The story diverges here once again. One telling says that the timepiece now embedded in his gut allowed Minuit to become a skilled clockmaker himself, the ever-present tick allowing him to keep a perfect sense of time and rhythm. The tale goes on to say that Fithian found love with a woman named Martha, after her seafaring father either chanced upon Minuit or came into his shop to have a chronometer repaired. The two men became friends, and, after the sea captain died, Fithian honored their friendship by marrying his daughter. In yet another added layer of the symbolism in this story, it was said that as long as the ticking continued inside Fithian, so would the love between Martha and him remain eternal. Pretty well-made piece of machinery to be stuck inside him for decades and not need any mainte-nance . . . I'm just saying.

Eventually, though, Fithian became a widower after Martha died many years later. She was buried in the graveyard that we can all visit today, next to the London Tract Church and just a stone's throw from White Clay Creek Preserve. Fithian continued to dutifully visit his wife's grave until he himself croaked, reportedly right on top of the grave during one of his regular trips there. Awfully poetic.

It was at this point that Fithian was buried alongside his beloved, and he must have loved her very much, because word began to spread that the ticking inside him continued on, even while he was 6 feet underground. I have gone there myself and pressed my ear to the ground in an effort to experience it, but to no avail. Maybe you have to believe in it more than I actually do. Or maybe any "ticking" that has been heard over the years is just a result of dripping rainwater into the ground or, more modernly, the vibration and rumble of nearby traffic.

On another note, Fithian Minuit and his wife, Martha, may not even be buried under the flat stone at all, since yet another differing version of the story says that one of Mason and Dixon's coworkers is the man taking up residence in the grave. He purportedly either stole or was given Dixon's chro-nometer (not Mason's, as in the previous telling) and then was either murdered or died of his own accord at some later time, was interred in the graveyard, and is the source of the ticking. Lots of variables here, and this legend does not even say that the watch is either on his person or in his stomach. So is the tick just a warning to all would-be thieves? Just when you thought this story could not get any more dubious, it does.

At the very least, while the name of this possible thief is lost to history, popular wisdom says that his initials were RC. And that's because, on the weather-worn slab of the Ticking Tomb, the letters "RC" can still be made out, which might completely blow up the version that says that Fithian Minuit is the real source of the ticking. We essentially have a grave for an unknown person or persons that may or may not emanate the sound of ticking if you dare to lower yourself to the ground to check it out. My head hurts.

The coup de grace of all this is the Ticking Tomb's connection, although tenuous, to the master of the macabre, Edgar Allan Poe. It is a point of fact that Poe spent some time in nearby Newark, Delaware, even managing to find time to put a curse on the Deer Park Tavern (then the St. Patrick's Inn) because he fell in mud on the street outside it. It is unknown if he ever took a jaunt up the road to visit the Ticking Tomb. Even if he didn't, perhaps he just heard the tale and became fascinated by it, because the theme of "ticking from a dead body down below" plays a crucial part in his short story "The Tell-Tale Heart."

The story, as most middle schoolers could probably tell you, involves a man driven mad by the perceived beating of his murder victim's heart after he shoved the man under the floorboards. It is similar enough to the Ticking Tomb to give some merit to the idea of the two tales being linked, especially with an imagination like Poe's at the helm. In actuality, Poe was probably mostly or exclusively inspired by the murder of Captain Joseph White at the Gardner-Pingree House in Salem, Massachusetts, in 1830.

The sensational trial that followed the murder featured Senator Daniel Webster as a prosecuting attorney. Webster's closing statement ended up being published into a pamphlet, enthralling all who read it. This included Poe, who seems to have used it as a springboard for much of the narration in "The Tell-Tale Heart." And so, in all likelihood, the Ticking Tomb did not elbow its way into the mind of Edgar Allan Poe, despite its timeline and location. Still, do not let this ever stop you from hyping up the legend if you feel the need to captivate an out-of-towner.

If you go, the Ticking Tomb can be found just a few paces from the northeast corner of the church building, which is now an office for the state park. You can reach the tomb by taking the short sidewalk between a break in the stone wall, continuing on to the grass, and then making a left after the first row of headstones. As mentioned, it is flat, but the roughly heart-shaped stone next to it will help you locate it. If you decide to go after dark, that's up to you to run the cost/benefit analysis of legality versus potential spookiness. Just don't say that I told you to do it.

No matter what you think of it, everyone can agree that the Ticking Tomb is in a beautiful area that is a fittingly representative image of Chester County as we know it. And every opportunity for a random Poe connection will always perk up the ears of certain people. Ultimately, I would recommend dropping by the tomb at least once, getting low, concentrating, and giving it a listen. Even if you don't hear anything unusual, you may still find yourself coming back again there someday. Time after time.

# Potter's Field

Location: 1722 Embreeville Road, Coatesville
39.93761, −75.72992

A fascinating albeit sad bit of history lies in plain sight at the ChesLen Preserve. And although this particular potter's field is far from unique, its story should be told and remembered by the local community.

Potter's fields in general have a long and interesting history, dating to the Bible itself, when the OG potter's field of Akeldama was supposedly constructed on a site that was either paid for by the money that Judas Iscariot received for betraying Jesus, or that Judas died and spilled his blood upon. No matter the origin, these mass graveyards have historically been used to inter foreigners, prisoners, wards of the state, or really any type of person who did not have family that could handle burial arrangements on their behalf. A sorrowful but necessary state of affairs for sure.

Although potter's fields are usually thought of as being found in and around large cities, rural Chester County contains one along the West Branch of the Brandywine Creek near Embreeville. That is because this was the site of the Chester County Poorhouse, which was also at various times called the Chester County Almshouse, the Chester County Home, and a number of other names throughout its history. And where you have institutionalized persons living and ultimately dying, you will of course need to have a place to bury the dead. Thus, a cemetery was created near the poorhouse.

Oh, and all this was happening more than two hundred years ago.

Eventually, enough residents of the poorhouse died that a new, larger cemetery had to be established in the 1890s. The poorhouse complex was expanding around this time so that they could add an asylum, and construction unearthed many human remains. These were moved to the new cemetery, where they would finally rest in peace. But Father Time remains undefeated, since the need for another new cemetery arose just a few years later, in about 1908. Set farther away from the hospital in a nature preserve, patients/inmates of the asylum were buried here under small, slightly angled headstones that featured only a number carved into the face of the rock—a final dehumanizing blow to these unfortunate individuals. And these are the stones that you can visit and pay your respects to today.

Burials continued in this third cemetery for about forty years, and we will likely never know the identities of those resting below. Any official records have been lost to history. As for the second cemetery, it is overgrown and inaccessible, off somewhere in the woods.

It is not an uplifting story in any way—a piece of the past that many would find best to acknowledge and then move on from rather quickly without reflecting too deeply on it. Unsurprisingly, there are no large, gaudy "THIS

WAY TO THE POTTER'S FIELD" indicators to lead you to the stones, with the site marked only by a simple wooden sign adorned with a small cross and yellow lettering that says: "Potters Field Est. 1800. Known but to God. Respected by us." Off to the side is a trail marker that reads:

Remnants of the Past

This cemetery—known as a "potter's field"—is a remnant of the Chester County Poorhouse, once located nearby. It contains several hundred graves where early residents of the poorhouse are buried.

Built in 1798, the poorhouse was a place of refuge for orphans and indigent adults. Its construction represented a vast improvement in the treatment of paupers, who, less than a century earlier, were forced to wear a scarlet "P" on their sleeves and risked being beaten or driven out of the county. The poorhouse expanded over the years to include an asylum for the mentally ill. It eventually became the Embreeville State Mental Hospital, which remained in operation until 1980.

This marker also features a photo of the area from the turn of the twentieth century, as well as a short paragraph about a woman known as "Indian Hannah," who is a notable figure in this story. Hannah was said to have been the last living member of the Lenni Lenape tribe until her death at the poorhouse on March 20, 1802. And although this assertion as the "last of her people" was most likely

false, it did come with the benefit of allowing the local white settlers to stake their claims on unoccupied land in the area for themselves, since there were no more native people around. Sadly, it appears that the government had placed Hannah, a respected healer and elder in the Native American community, in the poorhouse for the final years of her life for the express purpose of creating a sort of paper trail for them to gobble up more land after she died.

Hannah was buried in the first potter's field; it is unclear as to where exactly her remains are now, or even if they were among those moved as the facility expanded over the years. She does, however, have a grave marker in a wooded area near Stargazers Road, which takes about a mile of driving or walking to reach if you wanted to visit it after seeing the most recent potter's field.

In another interesting wrinkle of Chester County history, Hannah's marker is just a few hundred feet from the Star-Gazers' Stone (hence the name of the nearby road), which our old pals Mason and Dixon stuck in the ground there in 1764. It was in this general area that the surveyors constructed an observatory that functioned as their headquarters as they plotted their eponymous line. The Star-Gazers' Stone was used to mark the spot that was exactly 15 miles north of the border between Maryland and Pennsylvania, which was the famed pair's primary reason for being there in the first place. If you park in the lot near the ChesLen Preserve to visit the potter's field, you can walk in the opposite direction to lay your eyes on this handiwork of theirs.

As a final note on Hannah, she also has a monument near the entrance to Longwood Gardens, said to be the area in which she was born. This is the second location of said monument, which consists of a bronze plaque affixed to a granite boulder. It was created in 1925 and then relocated and rededicated at its current, more prominent spot in 2009. It is fitting that Hannah is honored in such a way, but the words "The Last of the Indians in Chester County" that appear on the monument really sting when placed in proper historical context.

The ChesLen Preserve is a beautiful place and is worth a visit, especially for those nature-inclined types who have yet to make the trek there. This author personally has visited it only in the bleakness of winter, but I am looking to go back and see it in full bloom. Its unassuming potter's field should be one of your stops during your time at ChesLen, although many visitors to the area probably are not even aware of its existence, since it is given only a passing mention on their website that simply regurgitates the information from the historical marker. But, like a lot of things, dig deep enough (figuratively) and you are likely to find elements of a hidden past. There is nobody famous or notable underfoot at this location, but that does not mean they should not be remembered. It honestly feels like the least we can do.

The easiest way to get to the cemetery is to park at the north end of the preserve in a small lot next to the Newlin Township Public Works building on Embreeville Road. From there you will take a stroll across the road and then across a short walking bridge that was built in 1908, according to the marble slab embedded within its stones at the midway point. No doubt this bridge used to accommodate carriages and early automobiles, but it is strictly for access to the walking path now. Another ten minutes or so of winding your way down the trail will get you to the clearing where the potter's field is located.

As for the buildings that sheltered these poor souls while they lived, much of the Embreeville hospital complex still stands today, although "stands" is a loose term, as its structures slowly succumb to decay and disuse, serving as a waypoint for oddity seekers, graffiti artists, squatters, and the like. There is, bluntly, an air of death about the area, even as nature steadily reclaims what man has done.

When I first visited the potter's field in 2023, there was another sign there that read "Restoration in Progress." Natural Lands—the nonprofit that runs ChesLen—had just received a grant to develop "20 acres of native pollinator meadows," which included the area surrounding the cemetery. As such, a beautification project was underway to level out the gravestones, remove invasive plants, and eventually create a wildflower meadow with a path that leads to the potter's field. It sounds like, maybe, the 204 individuals resting under the simple stones of the potter's field may not be forgotten after all.

# Duffy's Cut

Location: Behind a neighborhood off North Sugartown Road, Malvern
40.03704, −75.53201

Nearly two centuries after the tragedy that occurred there, we still do not know exactly what happened at Duffy's Cut. And, truth be told, some of the fateful events of the summer of 1832 will probably remain forever shrouded in mystery.

The Pennsylvania state historical marker that recognizes the event was placed at the intersection of West King Road and Sugartown Road in Malvern in 2004, and it succinctly tells the tale:

> Duffy's Cut Mass Grave
>
> Nearby is the mass grave of fifty-seven Irish immigrant workers who died in August 1832 of cholera. They had recently arrived in the United States and were employed by a construction contractor, named Duffy, for the Philadelphia and Columbia Railroad. Prejudice against Irish Catholics contributed to the denial of care to the workers. Their illness and death typified the hazards faced by many nineteenth-century immigrant industrial workers.

A terrible tragedy, but one not altogether uncommon at the time. Except there is very possibly much more to this story. And we will need to go back to 1832 to start sussing things out. Duffy's Cut gets its name from a man named Philip Duffy, who hired the fifty-seven ill-fated workers to complete a particularly grueling job of clearing a mile-long stretch of tough terrain to pave the way for the new railroad. Irish immigrants, arriving in massive numbers to the United States, were an easy target for men like Duffy, who saw them as only a means to an end rather than actual human beings. You would think that Duffy, an Irish immigrant himself, would have given more than a fleeting concern about his industrious countrymen, but he did not. It was all about cheap labor.

The stretch of land that needed to be cleared for this project of the Philadelphia and Columbia Railroad, mile 59, would require intensive manual labor to excavate sections of earth and essentially use it to fill in a chasm to bridge areas that were at higher elevations. As Watson and Watson (2018)—whom we will get back to shortly—explain, "The fill consisted of the rocks and soil that had been grubbed from the 'cut' and taken by cart and dumped where the earthen bridge was to be located. It was an arduous, backbreaking effort undertaken by men and horses in a manner that would not have differed much from the way such work was done in antiquity" (p.

21). As a result, it would come at a great cost to the railroad company, meaning that Duffy stood to make a hefty profit if his men could complete the work in a timely fashion.

They did not.

Initial work in the area had begun the previous year (1831), with an agreed-upon completion date of April 1, 1832. That day came and went, and it was in June 1832 that the *John Stamp* arrived in Philadelphia, carrying the fifty-seven Irish immigrants who would all be dead within eight weeks. These men were hired by Duffy and they worked until August, which is when tragedy struck. But just what kind of tragedy we can't be definitively sure.

The original story says that all the men contracted, then died of, cholera. A local blacksmith and some nuns in the area did their best to comfort the sick, but to no avail. As horrible as the whole situation was, it was not unusual, with public health standards being what they were during this period of history. There was an ongoing epidemic at the time, and these laborers were particularly susceptible, working literally in the dirt and within close quarters of one another. Once the sickness began raging among them, the men were quarantined, and the end result was that they all perished. We will get back to the circumstances of their deaths, but the first mystery of Duffy's Cut pertained to where the men were actually buried.

Many assumed that they had been placed near a wall by the tracks. Others believed that the bodies were put in with the railroad fill itself, which is terrible to think about but is on par with the fact that people's bodies are known to be part of structures, such as the Hoover Dam, as a result of construction accidents. Or perhaps the bodies were given more-fitting burials out in the valley, away from the immediate area of the railroad. Nobody knew the actual truth.

There was another version of the story, one that lingered under the surface for many years but that had no proof to back it up until researchers and scholars at nearby Immaculata University founded the Duffy's Cut Project in 2002. Spearheaded by brothers J. Francis and William Watson, whose grandfather had worked for the Pennsylvania Railroad and passed on to them a secret file from its archives regarding the events of 1832, the Duffy's Cut Project began to make inroads into finally solving this mystery. This partnership was responsible for the placement of the aforementioned historical marker and, more importantly, sought to excavate the site to learn more about what happened and, it was hoped, to give more-fitting burials to some of those who were victims of this event.

After several years of meticulous digging that unearthed a multitude of artifacts and the remnants of the worker's shanty, which was supposedly burned to the ground in the aftermath of the tragedy, the first human bones at the site were found in 2009. Many featured signs of blunt force trauma, seemingly confirming the suspicion that the history of Duffy's Cut was even darker than the accepted version of the story.

As more and more bones turned up, it fed the new narrative that as cholera rampaged among the men, some of them (perhaps most of them) were killed by locals who were afraid of the disease being spread to the greater community. It certainly did not help matters that the Irish immigrants were viewed so poorly by American society at the time, either, so we could be dealing with mass hate crimes on top of this. Any offenders no doubt felt that they had multiple reasons to commit such unspeakable acts against the Irish workers, whom they viewed as a plague. No matter the actual motives, these discoveries marked a tonal shift in the entire way that Duffy's Cut would be viewed going forward.

The Duffy's Cut Project is ongoing as of this writing, and it has done much good to excavate and then reinter some of the victims. Five reburials occurred in 2012 at Laurel Hill West Cemetery in Bala Cynwyd, and two other sets of remains were returned to their native Ireland for reburial: a widow named Catherine Burns, who was traveling with her father-in-law, and a young man named John Ruddy. With researchers working from the passenger list of the men known to have come to Duffy's Cut after traveling on the *John Stamp*, Ruddy was positively identified thanks to a rare dental abnormality, which DNA testing showed to be still present in his modern descendants. Truly amazing work.

On the basis of the fact that only a small number of bodies were unearthed together (many of them entwined within the roots of a tree) and showed forensic evidence of violent deaths, Watson and Watson (2018) conclude that these individuals were the first ones killed by locals after fleeing their camp due to the cholera outbreak. "It is likely that the first seven workers—who were healthy—broke out of a quarantine established by the Horse Company at mile 59 and were rounded up and murdered off-site by blunt[-]force trauma and gunfire" (p. 146). What percentage of the remaining laborers died by violence versus disease is hard to say, but this initial assertion seems to be indisputable.

As for Philip Duffy, the namesake of this tragedy, he was nowhere to be found at the time. After learning of what had happened, he of course hired even more men to complete the work, never giving much indication how he felt about dozens of people dying / being murdered on his watch (or lack thereof). Ultimately he would go on to a successful career with the railroad and some political dabblings. He died in 1871, after a long and prosperous life. Things are hardly ever fair, are they?

On the paranormal side of things, Duffy's Cut has inspired sightings and stories almost from day one after the tragedy. Green and blue ghosts were reported in the area, attributed to the fact that the unfortunate Irish were not buried via a proper religious ceremony. Without this, their spirits were said to be doomed to walk the earth, unable to rest.

Numerous other tales have cropped up in the nearly two centuries since, with reports ranging from nearby residents seeing phantom workers outside their windows at night to one eyewitness seeing an unexplained ball of light crossing the road very close to the historical marker on Sugartown Road. The area also seemed to spawn a sort of evil as well, with several derailments near Duffy's Cut having been brought about deliberately by someone placing something on or vandalizing the tracks, possibly in an attempt to loot a wrecked train after obtaining information that there was a sizable amount of money on board.

Immaculata University continues to be a driving force in the effort to uncover the truth of what happened. In 2005, even before any human remains had been found, an array of artifacts were put on display at the university library. It included tools and belongings of the railroad workers, as well as pieces from the blacksmith's shed, where many of the sick men were cared for and supposedly drew their final breaths. In the presence of these objects, strange occurrences took place, such as electronics turning on and off on their own and unexplained knocking on doors and windows.

Visiting the actual site is tricky, since it lies in a wooded area near the railroad tracks and behind private property that you would presumably need to walk through to access. I may or may not have cut between two houses to get a glimpse of the site from atop a small hill when I made a trek out to the area. The rectangular stone enclosure—circa 1909—roughly outlines where the original wooden fence was first placed in 1872 or 1873, and a metal sign suspended overhead in 2017 (replacing an earlier one) states that this is the burial plot of the Irish railroad workers.

It will be difficult to piece together the entirety of what happened in this secluded area nearly two hundred years ago, but archeological findings and forensic examination strongly indicate that more than mere disease was at play. These newly arrived immigrants were worked hard, got sick, and in all likelihood were summarily discarded by the very society that they had come to be a part of. Any further digging is halted for the time being, thanks to the proximity of Duffy's Cut to the vital Amtrak line that runs through the area. It is anyone's guess as to when that will ever be ironed out.

On top of all this, there are also mass graves of Irish workers in Downingtown and Spring City that may be subjected to further research in the near future. Could these also be not just burial plots, but mass murder sites? Time will tell. As for Duffy's Cut, we are left with only a partially solved mystery and the ghostly echoes that reside in the area even generations later.

# Pennhurst State School and Hospital

Location: 250 Commonwealth Drive, Spring City
40.19326, −75.56102

More than any other locale discussed in this book, Pennhurst State School and Hospital (alternately known as "Pennhurst Asylum" if you are trying to be sensational about it) has received the greatest amount of notoriety over the past few decades. And naturally, most of the reasons behind the great public interest in this crumbling complex are not good. Now it exists as a morbid point of fascination for many, one that offers some spine-tingling events during the "spooky season"—events that a lot of people are not on board with because of the dark, sad history held within its walls.

Before the "Pennhurst" moniker came along some fifteen years later, the facility's original given name was the Eastern Pennsylvania State Institution for the Feeble-Minded and Epileptic, which is really jarring and should sicken you right off the bat. Sadly, the horrible situation there and the atrocities within were not widely known for many years. Either that, or people simply preferred not to think about it until local reporter Bill Baldini finally held up a mirror to the situation when he created a five-episode documentary called *Suffer the Little Children* in 1968. These were the kinds of things never seen before on the relatively new medium of television—disabled and disturbed patients/inmates living in squalid conditions, locked away by a society that had discarded them because they did not understand them or were not willing to help.

At this point, Pennhurst had been operating for some fifty years, and the documentary turned out to be the flash point that would bring about its end, although it would still take two decades even after the public was finally forced to confront what was happening in their own backyard. At its peak the institution housed some 2,700 human beings, far more than it was capable of providing the necessary support for.

The idea behind Pennhurst, and places like it, was flawed from the very beginning. The authorities sought to separate and isolate a certain segment of the population, and people were banished to these kinds of institutions by society. That way, the thinking went, they would be protected and comfortable, while they also could not cause any disruptions among the "normal" population. It was a win-win situation in the mentality of the day, with its inherent inhumanity not registering at the time.

Still, for decades things persisted at Pennhurst, with its residents badly in need of a support system that they clearly were not getting. Most staff members did whatever they could to help the situation, although a few of them no doubt contributed to the misery of the place. They were, by and large, a group of dedicated people who had the patients' best interests in mind, but who were largely underfunded and did not have the necessary resources at their disposal. As a result, predictably, suffering was plentiful at Pennhurst.

Disease was rampant, largely due to severe overcrowding, with scourges such as tuberculosis and hepatitis chief among them. Preventive care was also not available, with patients receiving treatment at the hospital only after they had already become demonstrably ill. One of the great ironies in all of this was the fact that the unpaid labor of the residents themselves (gardening, food service, laundry, etc.) was crucial to keep Pennhurst humming along. The warm bodies of the occupants were needed to support the very place in which they would most likely be trapped for the rest of their lives, because Pennhurst could not continue to exist without their large, free contributions.

Perhaps the saddest element of Pennhurst is the fact that it also functioned as a school, acting both as a teaching institution and a prison of sorts for developmentally disabled children. Through no fault of their own, many of these children would spend their entire lives at Pennhurst—reared and educated there, working there, dying there. The fact that some people would never be "given a chance" among the general population is more disheartening, at least in my mind, than society locking away an adult that they deemed to be "too much of a problem to deal with." The point is, if you like misery, Pennhurst had it in spades.

All told, more than ten thousand people passed through the doors of Pennhurst during the roughly seventy years that they admitted new patients/inmates. And it took until Bill Baldini's exposé to get the ball rolling on transitioning away from the model that had been in place at Pennhurst for far too long. Pennhurst finally shut its doors for good in 1987, and its thousand-plus residents at the time were relocated to state-run housing. In the decades since, renovations have occurred to some of the campus, while much of it has been demolished, too far gone to salvage and too stained with anguish for anyone to want to save it even if they could.

Today, a portion of what remains operates in its well-known, somewhat infamous form as a top Halloween attraction in the region, with live actors the key to making it sometimes outrageously shocking. Many of the performers have disabilities themselves, and some even have lived within institutions in the past, giving credence to the idea that at least some of the population who would seemingly be the most offended by Pennhurst's continued existence does not object to the spectacle that it has been turned into. Is it objectively offensive and disrespectful to those who lived and died there? I suppose it just depends on how each individual person chooses to view it.

And there is the graveyard, of course, where a number of Pennhurst's inhabitants ultimately ended up. It is surprisingly small, tallying about a hundred graves, since it was used only from 1918 (starting with a few "Spanish flu" victims) into the early 1930s. Still, this small cross section of Pennhurst residents is representative of the whole. They were shut away and made to simply pass the time until they were no longer society's problem. Originally these poor souls rested under gravestones that carried only numbers, but this was rectified in 1978, when new markers showing their names were installed.

Ghosts? Of course. There are many reports of spectral happenings, primarily in the forms of cries of anguish and pain from the spirits of the unfortunate who spent large portions of their lives there. People have also heard voices yelling phrases such as "I'll kill you!," "Why did you come here?," and "Why won't you leave?" Other entities have been spotted hiding behind furniture or other objects to avoid torment from those who abused them at the facility. They remain fearful, even in death. Investigators have been pushed and scratched, and they have seen objects go flying through the air. And according to the Travel Channel's always reputable *Ghost Adventures*, "There are reports of slamming doors, footsteps, and sounds of vomiting coming from otherwise empty rooms. Some witnesses have seen the spirit of a little girl roaming the buildings, perhaps waiting to tell her own story of sorrow and neglect."

Over at the uber-haunted Mayflower Building, the ghost of a young boy named Howie is said to get upset when you touch the toy airplane that he left in one of the rooms. Meanwhile, a shadowy figure elsewhere in the building has been dubbed "Fisher" because the name is carved on the wall of one of the rooms. And the spirit of a nurse also throws off some very negative vibes in the Mayflower, giving some investigators the feeling that they are being poked with needles. With so much activity going on, it has basically been open season for any paranormal team who has investigated Pennhurst.

For the rest of you, if you ever visit Pennhurst, please go only during sanctioned times and events, since the place is very clearly marked with warnings about trespassing. It is also far enough from any main road that you are not going to make a quick getaway if something happens, either. It is not something that I would want to mess with personally, although a friend of mine went there a number of years ago under cover of night for some guerrilla filmmaking. He escaped unscathed, but you probably should not press your luck.

Today, we have a semioccupied, mostly ruined collection of buildings that seem to be stuck in the twilight zone between life and death. Pennhurst stands as an existing reminder of some startling instances of inhumanity that should not escape our consciousness anytime soon. As Pirmann (2015) puts it, "People with disabilities, intellectual and otherwise, do not need to live in a false world apart. They need what we all need—acceptance, friends, love and community" (p. 8). I hope that the presence of places such as Pennhurst means that we will never again forget this tenet of society. For now, you can go there around Halloween for a good scare. Just remember why it is there to begin with.

# Mad Anthony Wayne

Location: Old Saint David's Episcopal Church Cemetery, Devon
40.02728, −75.40468

This one gets pretty gross. Grisly even. General Anthony Wayne was a conquering hero of the American Revolution, one of George Washington's many dependable sidekicks who simply got stuff done and knew how to win a war. As such, his life and lofty accomplishments have been memorialized and celebrated in the centuries since his death, with statues having been erected in his honor and plenty of places named after him. He was even briefly a congressman, serving as a representative for Georgia, where he had moved after the war. His name will be remembered for as long as the United States of America exists as a nation.

But you are not here for that; you want to know what the deal was with his death and the ensuing tale of his mortal remains.

Shortly after Wayne was voted out of office by Congress due to an electoral-fraud scandal, George Washington decided to call upon Wayne once again for a military assignment. With the fledgling nation engaged in the largely forgotten Northwest Indian War, a border war with several Native American tribes, Wayne was named commander of the Legion of the United States.

General Wayne served in this role from 1792 until December 1796, when he found himself stricken with an acute case of gout at an army outpost in Erie, Pennsylvania, while on a return trip home to eastern Pennsylvania. Far from the nearest capable doctors, Wayne died from his affliction just before any help could arrive. Amazingly, Wayne was just fifty-one years old at the time of his death, although that essentially made him a geezer during that time period, and he had no doubt put some hard miles on his body.

Wayne's death had all the appearances of a natural occurrence, but some people have speculated that he was murdered by his scheming rival James Wilkinson, who was passed over for the commander job and made no "bones" about his envy. Given the fact that Wilkinson was promoted as a result of Wayne's death and then was later exposed as having been a spy for Spain some years after his own demise, there may be some credibility to the murder/power-grab idea, but it still remains conjecture to this day.

Speaking of bones, Wayne's earthly body was buried under the flagpole of the military blockhouse out in Erie, wearing his uniform and residing in a simple wooden box, per his wishes. General Wayne did not have any grandiose ideas about how he would spend his afterlife. He resided in Erie for more than a decade, and that would have been the end of it, but his children decided that it would be best to bring him back home to eastern Pennsylvania. Tellings of this story will say that the family plot was in Radnor, but it is actually in Devon, if you want to be technical about it.

In 1809, Wayne's daughter Margaretta was battling an illness that sadly would take her life at age thirty-nine shortly thereafter. In her final months she asked her younger brother, Isaac, to claim their father's body and bring him home. Isaac Wayne, a state senator who would later reach the rank of colonel during the War of 1812, granted his sister's dying request and took the long carriage ride across the state. Upon arriving in Erie, Isaac met with a Dr. Wallace (whom I have found being reported as having the first name of either John or James, or simply going by J. C.). Regardless of the moniker, Dr. Wallace was in fact one of the physicians who had arrived on the scene too late to help save the general's life thirteen years earlier.

Wayne's body was exhumed and found to be in surprisingly excellent condition, though one account by a local man, Henry Whitney, noted that "the flesh on his back bone was four inches thick solid and firm like new pork." That is . . . disgusting, but the body was in good shape overall, considering the circumstances. There was a problem, though. Isaac had no way of transporting his father's entire body in the carriage in which he had arrived. He was expecting his dad to be just a collection of dust by that point. And so he and Dr. Wallace decided to do what anyone would in this situation: dismember the desiccated corpse and boil the flesh off its bones. Duh.

Yes, the remains of a long-dead hero of the American Revolution were hacked up and tossed into a cauldron, where they were boiled until all the remaining skin and tissue sloughed off his bones, all in an effort to make him more easily transportable back to the family plot some 300 miles away. Wayne's stewed remains were reburied in the same spot in Erie, and it was a pretty unceremonious affair. The tools used during the boiling procedure were placed (or thrown) into the coffin with the general's uniform and the newly formed Wayne soup after the bones were scraped clean.

It is not known if Dr. Wallace, and whoever assisted him, carried the whole thing out with medical precision or if they were so disgusted by it that they hurried through. And maybe the instruments were not even buried, since tools have been put on display in the years since with the accompanying claim that they were the actual artifacts and not reproductions. Who knows for sure?

The cauldron used for this event is similarly in dispute, since an item fitting the bill has been on display by the Erie County Historical Society, along with the chair that Wayne was reported to have died in. It may be the most interesting thing you come across if you ever have to go to Erie. As to its authenticity, that also depends on whom you ask.

Getting back to the matter at hand, the bones of the dead-and-now-strained General Wayne were loaded into boxes or saddlebags to be placed in his son's carriage for the bumpy ride east. Along the way it is said that some bones fell out, littering the roadway, and not all of them were recovered. Even General Wayne's skull may have been a casualty of the journey, lost in the muck and probably crushed under a carriage wheel a short while after it had been boiled clean for reburial. You have to wonder where the facts stop and legend takes over.

Eventually, though, an acceptable amount of Wayne's bones made it back to Chester County to be interred in the family plot at St. David's Episcopal Church graveyard, where they rest today. The parts of Wayne that remained in Erie were dug up *again* in 1878, some years after the blockhouse where it was located had burned to the ground. The gravesite had been lost, and locals wanted to check and make sure they knew where it was. Mercifully, it has not been disturbed again since. What a ride.

Of course, on top of all of this there are the supposed hauntings and sightings of the ghost of "Mad" Anthony Wayne. The most prominent story says that Wayne's spirit can be seen riding on horseback on various points all throughout Pennsylvania, retracing the carriage route that carried him to his resting place as he searches for his bones. Some versions further state that Wayne's "bone ride" may occur only annually on January 1, which happens to be his birthday, as he rises from his grave (the one in Chester County) to start his quest anew.

The supernatural goes even further, since there have reportedly been disturbances at Waynesborough, the former Wayne family home, which is now a museum (2049 Waynesborough Road in Paoli). On more than one occasion, when it was still a private residence, dinner parties at Waynesborough were interrupted when all the women in attendance were startled by the sound of glass smashing, while none of the men heard a thing.

Far from being just another time when men were not listening, these situations were attributed to Hannah Wayne, a descendant of the general who died in a fire at the house in the middle of the nineteenth century after accidentally setting her clothes ablaze with a candle. As she tried to escape, screaming and with glass shattering all around her, all the men who lived and worked there were too far afield to hear the uproar. And so any instances of Hannah making her presence felt today continue to fall on deaf ears for any men in attendance. Yes, these encounters only indirectly involve Anthony Wayne, but they have happened under his former roof, so he at least gets partial credit for any residual spookiness.

Curiously enough, the bones of Anthony Wayne now rest for all eternity not in Wayne, the town that named itself in honor of him, but in Devon (there's that technicality I mentioned), since the dividing line between the two is formed by Valley Forge Road, which winds itself right past the front gate of Old Saint David's Episcopal Church cemetery. There, just a few paces off to the left, you will find the grave of General Wayne. At least you'll find the one that we care about for the purposes of this book. The man certainly packed a lot into his life, and his story postdeath has been even more interesting. And perhaps General Wayne is not done yet.

# What's Up with "the Wedge"?

While most of the borders between states here in the lower forty-eight were created by drawing straight lines on a map or simply following the curve of a river or other body of water, the arc that forms the entire southeastern portion of the Chester County line is a nice change of pace.

When the king of England granted a large swath of land to William Penn, which we now know as Pennsylvania, it bordered a plot of land belonging to the Duke of York that was measured as extending for 12 miles from the courthouse in Old New Castle (which was not so old back then) and then to points south, as in the rest of what we know today as the state of Delaware. The Penns later bought this land, establishing the "lower counties" of Delaware, which of course became the colony and then the state. The problem here was that the charter issued to Penn directly conflicted with a charter that had been issued to the Calverts of Maryland some decades earlier. As a result, a sizable strip of land below the fortieth parallel, including the city of Philadelphia, was now in dispute. Oops.

This led to decades of confusion and infighting, and even a series of violent events in 1736–37 that became known as "Cresap's War," so named after Maryland trader/ferryman Thomas Cresap, who was in the service of Lord Baltimore and operated businesses in Maryland and Pennsylvania. Cresap's shenanigans even earned him the nickname the "Maryland Monster" from irked Pennsylvanians. To make a long story short, militias from both colonies were called upon, and it was only after the king of England issued a proclamation that they knocked it off. Essentially, this laid the groundwork for the decision to call upon Charles Mason and Jeremiah Dixon a few years later to settle the matter once and for all regarding borders.

This is where the wedge finally comes into play.

So, picture the hand of a clock with its base at the Old New Castle courthouse in Delaware, making a counterclockwise sweeping motion and creating the rounded top of Delaware's border. At around 10:00 (still using the clock analogy here; stay with me) the circular border ends up creating a "gray area" between the border lines separating Pennsylvania and Maryland that Mason and Dixon surveyed and declared as official. Oops again.

Common sense prevailed, though, and the wedge was informally accepted as part of Delaware, if for no other reason than it would look stupid as a little sliver hanging off the eastern edge of Maryland. One could argue that it should be part of Pennsylvania, since it lay outside the 12-mile circle, but that did not really matter, since the Penns also owned Delaware at the time.

Then the whole "American Revolution" thing happened and we got states. Delaware and Pennsylvania were no longer joined at the hip, and technically the wedge was in dispute again. Without any fanfare, Delaware decided to keep it, and nobody seemed to mind until the area was surveyed again in 1849, and Pennsylvania got all worked up about it.

Keep in mind, this is 1.06 square miles of land.

Delaware paid Pennsylvania no heed, and the claim seemed to have been put to bed in 1892, when the Arc Corner Monument stone (39.7222, −75.7739, approximate address: 520 Hopkins Road) was laid by a US government office. Pennsylvania did not fully cede any claim to the wedge until 1921, meaning that it was kinda sorta part of Chester County in some people's minds until just a little over a century ago. At least nobody sent armed forces into the area over this, although sillier things have happened.

Today, most people will probably just think of slavery when any talk of the Mason-Dixon Line comes up. It is a sad truth, but it is not really the whole story. Far from it. Its roots actually came in the form of a land dispute, one that eventually had the trickle-down effect of creating the geographical anomaly we know as "the Wedge." To my knowledge, this small piece of land has never been the site of anything notable, but its mere existence merits an explanation when digging through the annals of area history. It is a part of Chester County that has quite literally been lost.

# TWO

## Ghosts and Legends around Town

From Phoenixville to West Chester, and in several other pockets of Chester County, you will find decent-sized metropolitan areas where there are more activities to keep you occupied, the living is pleasant, and you can get away from the feeling of being "out in the country," even if you are just passing through for a brief spell. Needless to say, these spots still contain their fair share of history and the lore surrounding it, and they are notable for physical places or the stories, or both, that have become part of the community.

An eerie old cemetery or a more rural locale probably feels a bit divorced from everyday life, like we have to go out of our way to examine it. But the following locations and stories are in or around population centers, basically within arm's reach of a sizable number of people.

Sometimes you have to dig a little deeper to find the haunted history of these places, but on other occasions it practically smacks you in the face, plain to see for any passerby. Let's examine some of the more "city-centric" haunts that can be found around Chester County.

# Exton Witch House

Location: Gordon Drive near Route 100, Exton (duh)
40.05786, −75.65021

This is a legend that doesn't have a whole lot of historical basis and may be one of the more shaky or questionable entries in this book if you are a skeptic to begin with. Still, it's gained legs over the last few years, and it merits mentioning in any complete dive into Chester County lore.

It's difficult to find a creditable source for the vague stories that surround this old farmhouse, which belonged to the Ferrell family some 150 years ago. Details are sketchy when it comes to when exactly it was built and what, if anything, unsavory happened there. But you know how people love their legends, as locals somehow adopted the idea that the house was a center for witchcraft activity.

It is said that the entire family of four (mom, dad, and two kids) died around the same time in the late nineteenth century. Was this a wave of sickness that decimated the family, or something more sinister? Could it have been related to their alleged witchcraft? Presupposing the latter, the family was interred on the property in a purported "witch's burial," standing straight up underground. But the graves of Jessie, Mary Jane, Annie, and Walter Ferrell are no longer on their former property today. Even their headstones were removed some years ago to keep them from being vandalized into oblivion. The family now rests eternally at Fairview Cemetery in Coatesville. What's more, the death dates given on their shared stone do not coincide with the whole family dying at or around the same time, since they are spread out over some thirty years. So much for them all mysteriously dying together, I suppose.

And that's essentially the story. If the Ferrell family really was a coven of witches, we don't know any details about the kinds of practices they engaged in—or how said practices or their dark master himself may have brought about their deaths. Frankly, the whole truth of the Exton Witch House might just be that someone decided, "That old building is cool and creepy, so there must be a story behind it."

You're not going to find much documentation in any reputable sources, either, even as far as ghosts and lore are concerned. That's somewhat of a bummer when it comes to these types of things, but it's not uncommon or surprising. Unsubstantiated rumors also say that the Ferrell farmhouse was used by the Underground Railroad, with a tunnel connecting it to one of the other buildings on the property. Maybe this bit is accurate, which would lend the place much more historical significance, but there doesn't seem to be any way to prove it. Either way, the sheer oddity of this early American edifice still standing in the middle of a very modernized and suburban area is at least notable in and of itself, making it an appropriate target for curiosity seekers.

Barely visible through a thicket of trees across from a hotel, the house has been nicely restored over the past few years, hugely upgraded from the decaying structure that you can find some "urban explorers" perusing in a few online videos that were posted in the 2010s. Presumably the interior also matches its spiffy new look. And, as it turns out, access to the place is actually easier than previously thought, with the house closer to an industrial park on the other side of the road than to the nearby hotel through the woods. Some of the explorers in these videos have reported hearing phantom screams and seeing a sort of floating mist or ghostly mass in the area, largely attributing these phenomena to the Ferrell family. But the spectral happenings at this place don't go much further than that.

Thanks to the witch house's fresh facade, you'll just have to live vicariously through the old online videos that show the house in its dilapidated form, heavily graffitied, with windows completely boarded up. You may even get an extra kick out of the way that some trespassers—I mean "urban explorers"—have set their videos and still images to ominous music to really crank up the atmosphere on the place. It's almost as chilling as some of the misspellings in the videos. In all honesty, though, you aren't going to see or find out a whole heck of a lot by watching any of what's out there, and much of the allure has now been removed by the recent renovations. As far as Chester County lore goes, this supposed witch house seems to be a minor player until anything more materializes, which it probably won't.

# Phoenixville Library

Location: 183 2nd Avenue, Phoenixville
40.12885, −75.51412

Libraries, in general, seem like as good a place as any for your local spooks, specters, and spirits to take up residence. They are often old, historical structures, and the air of silence about them just seems to lend itself to an unsettling feeling that something unseen lurks around the next bookshelf. I mean, just look at the very first scene of *Ghostbusters*. There are probably a bunch of people who needed to change their pants before the opening title sequence.

At the Phoenixville Library that is exactly what seems to be the case, since they have a rather large number of ghosts jammed into the facility. At its roots, the Phoenixville Library started as a subscription library in the 1800s, when it began to loan out books from the collection of a local church pastor. When Pennsylvania created its public library system in 1896, the Public Library of Phoenixville was officially established, and efforts turned toward raising money to erect a brand-new building, the one that we know today.

Help came from superrich Andrew Carnegie, who was spitting out dollars for the building of libraries left and right. With the funding secured, the new library was constructed, and it opened its doors in 1902. As you would expect, it grew, expanded, and changed along with its surrounding community over the years, and a quick scan of the timeline on the library's website can fill you in on all those details. What the site does not get into—and which you have to look elsewhere for—are accounts of the paranormal. And there are a bunch.

It was during the latter half of the twentieth century that, for whatever reason, people working in and visiting the library began to describe their experiences of having an odd sensation of being watched or otherwise sensing that they were accompanied by some unseen presence. An executive director at the time waved these away as hokum, until he himself saw "a book jump off the shelf and felt a wind coming up my back as I came through the security gate" (Roseberry 2007, 50). He also reported that one of the staff members always avoided certain portions of the building because of a presence that they sensed in those areas.

One of the main manifestations in question here is a bearded man with a dog, which is as much information as they have been able to discern and report. The same executive director also stated that he encountered a different man, an older one this time, among the stacks when the library was not busy. He found himself suddenly in the presence of this man in one of the aisles, then the man was gone just seconds later, with no explanation behind it. The executive director asked other staff members if they had spotted this individual, but no one had seen him enter or exit the building.

The children's library, on the bottom floor of the building, has shown spectral evidence of a young girl. One far-flung conjecture is that the girl was an escapee who had passed through this area when it was once part of the Underground Railroad. She has been heard whistling, perhaps waiting for her mother, from whom she had become separated so many years ago.

Other unexplained occurrences have taken place at the building's security gate, which works as a sort of electronic turnstile, emitting a small clicking noise as a person breaks an invisible beam and passes through it. This should send out a single click, but more than one click has been heard on numerous occasions, trailing immediately behind a visitor or staff member. Malfunctioning equipment or roaming entities? You make the call.

There are still more disturbances here. One employee felt a tapping on her shoulder and a disembodied voice saying, "Hi" to her when she was otherwise alone. Leaning on this encounter, South Jersey Ghost Research has taken many photos that show floating orbs in them, possible indicators of an energy in the area. There is also said to be a middle-aged woman in the attic who may or may not be responsible for some tremendously loud crashing noises that never turn up anything physical when staff go to the attic to "check things out" (library pun).

There have also been tales of books dropping/flying off the shelves on their own, which you would fully expect in a haunted library, as well as a general feeling of unease in the Carnegie Room. It seems as if some unseen spirit has given staff members the idea that they are unwelcome, which has caused many of them to steer clear of the area.

As a result of all these happenings, the Chester County Paranormal Research Society has conducted multiple investigations of the library. Society members have felt a presence, caught strange shadows on camera, and even managed to get a video of a book falling on its own. Most of their discoveries came in the attic space, where an unseen presence was sensed by their equipment. "All who feel the entity in the attic, including the Jersey team, say that the spirit there is a playful one. This team took many photographs in the attic, and spirit orbs were visible everyplace in their photographs" (Roseberry 2007, 60). An episode of a paranormal program was also filmed during a 2009 visit by a different "ghost hunter" crew, and you can watch the results online and decide for yourself what you think of the residual energy that they claim to have come across during their time at the library.

Add this all up and the Phoenixville branch certainly seems to offer up way more activity than any of the other libraries dotting the landscape of Chester County. And I don't just mean movie nights and toddler time.

# The Ghost
# in the Clock Tower

Location: 2 North High Street, West Chester
39.95973, −75.60509

The borough of West Chester is the venerable seat of the county, home to the titular local university, and the place where you have to go if you are unlucky enough to be summoned for jury duty or have other legal matters to attend to. The building where this all happens is the menacingly named Chester County Justice Center, a modern brick-and-concrete edifice on West Market Street that first opened its doors in 2008 to serve the people.

It was built to replace the aging structure some three blocks down at the corner of West Market and North High Streets, the Historic Chester County Courthouse. Opened in either 1846 or 1847 to replace the previous courthouse, which had been operational since 1786, two additions were built in later years, and the old courthouse was a bustling center for legal proceedings in its heyday. Even today it is not just some relic, since it still houses the county treasurer and a number of other offices, as well as functioning as a space for special events. It seems like the kind of old building that would be perfectly suited for paranormal visits within its walls, but our interests lie above the main floors, in the cupola and clock tower that sit perched above it.

The story of the ghost in this clock tower can be found referenced in a few places, but it seems to have been passed down mostly orally over the years. At the Chester County Community Foundation, community engagement officer Malcolm Johnstone spins the tale of how the courthouse clock was an integral part of the community in a time before personal clocks, watches, and cell phones. Yes, there was a time when those did not exist, kids.

As Mr. Johnstone explains, a few years before the Civil War the clock began to ring erratically one chilly morning and would not stop. The towns-people, stirred from their homes and alarmed, went to investigate the matter, with local officials and the clock keeper entering the courthouse. Said Mr. Johnstone in his video telling of the legend, "Upon arrival at the base inside the tower, where the only door was located, the clock keeper tried to open it. But he found that it was not only locked, but locked from the inside. Each man tried to force the door open, but it would not budge, and the clock tower continued to ring. Meanwhile, out on the street, an eerie dawn broke, shrouded by fog and bone-chilling cold."

It was at this point that locals saw smoke billowing from a cabin down the street, from which emerged a woman carrying her young daughter, followed by her husband, who ran back in to retrieve his son but then reemerged empty-handed. Sadly, rescue efforts were not successful, since the building went up in flames before the responders could get to the boy. His family, especially his mother, was inconsolable. All throughout this time the bell in the clock tower continued to ring, and the door leading up to it remained locked despite the best efforts of several men to pry it open. But then, just as all hope seemed lost, a child emerged from an alleyway; it was the young boy, whose parents grabbed him and held him tight. At this point—you guessed it—the ringing from the tower stopped.

Mr. Johnstone continues, saying, "The clock keeper tried one last time to try and [*sic*] unlock the door and curiously found that it opened easily, as if it had never been locked. Spending no time thinking about this new mystery, and bent on finding whomever [*sic*] was in there, the men climbed the last narrow flight of stairs to the inside workings of the clock. Everything was in order, with the clock simply ticking as always, with a slow but steady rhythm." There was no mystery intruder in the tower.

Locals concluded that the boy was awakened by the smoke from the fire and wandered outside, without his family realizing it, before he faced any danger, solving one of the puzzles. But officials were angered at the seemingly malfunctioning clock, still looking to put the blame on someone. When the crowd that had gathered was asked if any of them knew about the inner workings of the clock, a teenage boy volunteered that his grandfather had been the one to build it and was planning to teach him how to maintain it. The only problem was his grandfather had died the previous year.

The clock tower remains a stunning piece of architecture in downtown West Chester, although the original clock itself was said to have been replaced sometime in the first half of the twentieth century. But even if the clock we see today was not the exact same piece of machinery whose chimes stirred the townspeople all those years ago, the legend of the ghost in the tower persists. Was this the deceased builder of the original tower alerting the town to the fire and saving a potentially large loss of life? Or did the spirit have something to do with the fire starting in the first place, in a twist of poltergeist-like mischief? Or something in between? No answers have been given, even as the clock allegedly still chimes irregularly from time to time. It is a peculiar tale of how the unusual can arise from the most mundane and become fixed in local lore.

# Valley Creek Road Twin Tunnels

Location: Believe it or not, Valley Creek Road, Downingtown
40.00467, −75.66556

As you meander just off the beaten path outside the populated area of Downingtown, you may find yourself approaching the fabled "Twin Tunnels" of Valley Creek Road, which have become quite the subject of urban legends over the past few decades. Some of these stories definitely help the tunnels live up to the "dark and creepy roadway" reputation that they have managed to attain.

Constructed to support the railroad tracks that run overhead, the twin tunnels feel like a portal straight into *The Twilight Zone*, and they are also the kind of place where you might expect to find teenagers hanging around after hours. At least some of the mystique of the tunnels can be attributed to the efforts to construct them in 1912, as several laborers were buried alive when a section collapsed on them, giving the tunnels very distinct Duffy's Cut vibes right from the start. Things have only taken off since then. Stories abound, and one such tale says that a young woman who had given birth out of wedlock and had nowhere to turn once hanged herself from the air shaft above the tunnel. This would be sad enough in and of itself, but she decided to do so while holding her baby, which subsequently fell to its death once the mother plummeted to hers. As a result, a baby's cry is said to echo through the tunnels, calling out for someone to help it somehow escape the fate that has already befallen it.

If that is not eerie enough for you, it is a matter of public record that a grisly discovery was made in the creek alongside the tunnels in 1995. Authorities found a suitcase that contained the naked and dismembered body of a woman whom they were never able to positively identify despite their testing efforts. Given the location of where the body was found, people immediately began attributing the murder to the tunnels as either the site of the deed or the underlying sinister cause of it.

This unfortunate, unnamed woman is now said to call out for help to those who pass through the tunnels late at night. Depending on where you hear this story recounted, it has been perverted to say that a biker gang murdered some poor soul and then left her in a suitcase inside one of the tunnels, rather than in the water. It did not happen that way, but don't let facts get in the way if you want to put a sensationalistic spin on things. As one other bit of lore, there is also said to be a man who hanged himself in the tunnels and can be summoned if you stop your car in the tunnel and beep your horn. I do not know why you would do that, but have at it if you are so inclined. Or maybe you will spot another dark figure in the tunnels, as described by Nesbitt (2008): "A man beat his son to death and took his broken body to the tunnels to hide it. When the father died he was doomed to walk the tunnels forever, looking for the spirit of his lost son" (p. 31).

Another nod to the general creepiness of the area comes in the form of the tale of the gates at the entrance to Sawmill Road, which is a short distance away from the Twin Tunnels. Supposedly a pair of red cast-iron gates used to stand guard in front of a mansion that was both a murder site and a burying place for the victims. A man was alleged to have killed his entire family and then himself, and the whole lot of them are now tethered to the property for eternity. This area also, as always seems to be the case, is said to have hosted cults and other ritualistic gatherings. Today there are no gates to be seen; yet, the legend persists that this area is an actual portal to hell in the same vein that the twin tunnels are thought to be.

I found the twin tunnels pretty spooky the first time I drove through them, even during broad daylight. Once you see them up close, you understand why the place has become a hotbed of spectral activity, or at least speculation thereof. I might advise taking a different route, since the tunnels may detour you somewhere decidedly away from Valley Creek Road.

# THREE

Ghosts and Legends
in the Countryside

The legendary American band The Presidents of the United States of America once told us, "Moving to the country, I'm gonna eat a lot of peaches." Inspiring words, indeed. But, stone fruit aside, there sure is a lot of "country" in Chester County. And it is these types of areas, these open spaces of land, where some of the odder events, sightings, and bits of lore of Chester County have developed over the centuries.

There is just so much open, rolling space around the county that some out-of-the-ordinary or downright bizarre occurrences were bound to have happened there at some point over these last few centuries of civilization. From spooky rural roads to formerly bustling villages that are now sparsely populated, or abandoned altogether, a casual trek through Chester County gives you a good chance of stumbling upon something worthy of further study.

Haunted locales and ghosts of the past are part of the story, but not all of it, since there has just generally been some weird stuff that has occurred in the more bucolic areas of Chester County that has either been underreported to the masses or lost to history altogether. Let's take a Sunday drive around the county, shall we?

# The Dorlan Devil

Location: Near Marsh Creek Reservoir
40.04763, −75.71726

Cryptids, right? But "What is a cryptid?" you may ask. It is best to reference some examples to illustrate the point here, since creatures of lore such as the Loch Ness Monster and Bigfoot are the most prominent specimens that society has thrown at us in the last hundred years or so. Essentially, cryptids are beasts or beings that some (or many) believe in the existence of, but that have not been proven conclusively by science to exist in the wild, in the oceans, or anywhere else on our planet.

The most famous semilocal cryptid is the Jersey Devil. Its legacy dates back about 250 years, and its impact has been massive. Aside from the old-timey legends and occasional sightings that still occur, it has also been designated as the official state demon of New Jersey and been the naming inspiration for a hockey team, albeit a lousy one. It has spawned plenty of merchandise and some cool artwork and is a well-known pop culture touch point by now.

Where does Chester County come in here? Well, it has its own cryptid, known as the Dorlan Devil. The stories around it are loose and certainly not as well documented as its Jersey neighbor, but the Dorlan Devil merits mentioning in any search of the strange annals of Chester County history.

The first confirmed sighting of the DD, if you can call it that, came in 1932, in the general area of Dorlan, in Uwchlan Township. As is seemingly always the case with these sorts of things, details are fuzzy as to how many people witnessed something, and whether the person or persons were working in the area or simply passing by. At any rate, the story goes that a leaping creature of some sort appeared out of nowhere, "neither beast nor human," and scaring the bejesus out of the witnesses. Just as quickly this strange being scurried off, which prompted the witnesses to put together a search party to seek it out, probably with the goal of killing it. Nothing was ever turned up, and the creature did not even leave so much as footprints or paw prints for anyone to study further.

Reports of the Dorlan Devil's next appearance are better documented, since it reared its ugly head once again in July 1937. Three people were taking a drive in the area near where the southern portion of Marsh Creek Reservoir is now, when they suddenly came upon a hideous sight. Witness Cydney Ladley described it as an "oversized kangaroo with long black hair and eyes like red saucers." Sounds pretty chilling. And it also sounds a lot like certain renderings of the Jersey Devil, which is not surprising, given the human tendency to try to make ourselves comprehend something by drawing on the familiar when we see something so utterly unexpected.

People tend to get swept up in these kinds of waves. Call it mass hysteria if you like, or drinking the Kool-Aid, or whatever other phrase lends itself to the idea of our eyes and minds distorting things so that they conform to an idea or concept that we have come across before. The Salem witch trials, for instance. Those Puritans "made sense" of their situation by declaring that the devil had infiltrated their community, necessitating the elimination of those doing his bidding. It is an extreme example, yes, but studying bits of history like this helps us understand why people act the way that they do.

And so it is really not much of a reach to call the Dorlan Devil a byproduct of "Jersey Devil fever," with the added bonus that we got an alliterative name out of it. A brief trip through some lesser-known cryptids in J. W. Ocker's *The United States of Cryptids* gives us names such as the Glocester Ghoul, the Dover Demon, and the Beast of Busco. It seems to me that we would most definitely have the "Morlan Monster" or the "Torlan Terror," or some other double-consonant sound if town founders or mapmakers had simply ascribed a different name to Dorlan. It was low-hanging fruit for whoever coined the name.

And just to further prove my point, there is also an obscure "Devon Demon" in Chester County lore that dates to the mid-1800s and was allegedly the spirit of a man who was murdered at an inn that is today long gone. You've gotta love yet another use of alliteration here.

As for that 1937 sighting of the Dorlan Devil, the creature was said to have sprung across the road and out of sight. Once again, a posse was rounded up to search the swampland, but nothing was discovered. The Dorlan Devil has not been reported as reappearing since. In fact, the roadway along which it made itself known is now apparently underwater, a marshy area that has been claimed by Marsh Creek Reservoir in the decades since. We can't be sure if the Dev sprouted gills and took some swimming lessons, but it seems like it would have had to if it wanted to stay in the area.

Who can say what the Dorlan Devil even was? Or still is? A simple one-off of biology that had not existed before or since? An amalgam of light and shadow that witnesses mistook for something fantastical? A straight-up hoax? That is the allure of this. The Dorlan Devil, like all cryptids, cannot be conclusively proven as being false or made up. On the flip side, if its existence ever was confirmed, it ceases to be classified as a cryptid entirely, and any lingering fascination would be entirely drained away by the cold calculation of science.

The Dorlan Devil isn't exactly an A+ cryptid, but it seems to be the closest that Chester County has come to developing a legend along these lines. There won't be any festivals or statues in its honor anytime soon—a treatment that many cryptids around the country receive—but maybe some enterprising individual can expand on this story in the future to put it on the map. Thanks to technology, maybe we will even get a new round of sightings sometime to put some new life into the legend. Until then, just file this one away in the dustbin of Chester County history and chalk it up to a brief cryptid craze and some impressionable locals who just seemed to want some notoriety.

# The Pennypacker Tragedy

Location: About 1 mile east of Kimberton

Pennsylvania's history is rife with train wrecks. Morbid, I know, but it's just stating a fact. Ever since railways became an important way of moving people, livestock, and goods some 150 years ago, the law of probabilities, plus some very shoddy engineering in the early days of the industry, combined to produce some disastrous incidents.

In Chester County, the Pennypacker tragedy of October 4, 1877, was a particularly horrifying one.

The wreck in question occurred on the Pickering Valley Railroad, a short line of the Reading Railroad, near Phoenixville. Tragically, it occurred in the aftermath of a family reunion; hence why the "Pennypacker" name is attached to the event. Heinrich Pennypacker (which was the anglicized form of his original German surname, "Pfannebecker" or "Pannebecker") had been one of the first to settle in the area and became a pillar of the community. And though Heinrich had died more than a hundred years before the fateful night of October 4, 1877, his many descendants and their families (1,500 or so people) still came together to honor their heritage, which they did on that day in Schwenksville, despite heavy rains. The festive occasion wrapped up and all went their various ways, with many hopping on a train that was to carry them just a few miles home.

The first stop was in Phoenixville; the next leg of the journey had them traveling to Byers Station, which is near the town of Eagle. Some 130 or so folks were on this life-changing train ride, which came to an abrupt end as the train approached Kimberton, just a few miles west.

Due to the recent torrential storms in the area, the ground under some parts of the track had become unstable, leading to a large chunk of earth caving in. Upon reaching the area, the train immediately left the track, plummeting about 30 feet down into a chasm. The engineer and another worker in the locomotive with him were killed instantly, and the first two passenger cars tumbled into the gulf as well. The remaining cars of the train remained on the track, though these were only the baggage and milk cars, making one truly wonder about why the cars were attached in such an order. Should it have left the track with the passenger cars in the rear, any casualties would have been minimized, if not eliminated entirely.

There would be an inquest into the matter, but very little could be done. The extraordinary circumstances of the rain, with nearly 5 inches of it having fallen in a short period of time, washed away a good section of the track and compromised the ground so much that no real blame could be placed on anyone. A derailment was going to happen, though it was quite careless and confounding that the passenger cars had been hooked to the front of the train instead of the back, putting riders in unnecessary danger when the locomotive left the tracks. No one went to jail over it, but the jury did express their disapproval about the order of the cars, as well as the fact that iron bars were placed across the windows, making it impossible for people to break the glass to escape in the event of a catastrophe.

Dozens of people were injured; that much is not in dispute, but sources differ on just how many people died in the wreck, with anywhere from seven to twelve being the accepted range. Some, such as the unfortunate brakeman who was crushed between two cars, died almost instantly. But reports show that some lingered as late as October 8 (four days later), when information about the aftermath of the crash seems to dry up. More people could have eventually succumbed to their injuries, but we do not know for sure.

This derailment was, at the time, the worst in the history of Chester County. The Pickering Valley Railroad would continue operations for several more decades before fading away, just like the area's collective memory of the Pennypacker railway disaster, which cast a black cloud over it for years. Today you wouldn't know that anything of the sort had occurred here as you drive right on by where it happened.

# Free Love Valley

Location: Near Shenkel Road,
North Coventry Township
40.22365, −75.70407

Men and women cavorting naked in the countryside, engaging in "free love" practices, would be a shock to the system of many people. The 1960s? No, I'm talking about the middle of the nineteenth century in Chester County.

Welcome to Free Love Valley, site of a religious movement/cult that was well ahead of its time. Oh, and a brutal murder on top of that.

This strange series of events, and a generally underreported and bizarre chapter of Chester County history, can be traced to a preacher named Theophilus Gates. A fire-and-brimstone type of zealot, just as you were probably picturing him, Gates was a New Englander by birth who came to Philadelphia in 1810. It took decades for him to make his mark, but in 1837 he put out a pamphlet detailing his religious doctrine, titled "Battle-Axe and Weapons of War." Taking its name from a particularly fiery passage from the Bible's book of Jeremiah, the publication served to develop a following under Gates, with his devotees becoming known as the Battle Axes. Catchy.

Settling in North Coventry Township, in the far northern portion of Chester County, Gates and his small cadre of Battle Axes did their thing at their commune. Espousing their idea that marriage is for suckers, the residents of "Free Love Valley" instead preferred the "anytime, anywhere" approach when it came to states of undress and the pleasures that might be associated with it. They even supposedly walked or ran naked inside and around the local place of worship, Shenkel Church. This may have been part of one of their rituals or, in one specific case, a way to thumb their noses (and, one hopes, not any other body parts) at the local preacher who had been denouncing the Battle Axes to his congregation.

Still, by no means was this a satanic group, or one that otherwise threatened the communities beyond its reach. It was just . . . very different. And of course, such titillation was met with a good deal of opposition in proper and puritanical mid-nineteenth-century America.

In 1844, quite predictably, several members of the community were arrested and put on trial for their crimes of adultery and for breaking other indecency statutes. Some were acquitted, but a few were imprisoned after they admitted to their unwholesome activities—a cautionary tale for those who dared to continue such a lifestyle. Not too long after, Gates kicked the bucket.

He is currently resting at Oak Grove Cemetery in Spring City, in case you ever wanted to stop by. But his death did not serve to put an immediate end to the Battle Axes, since his acolyte Hannah Williamson took up the mantle as the group's leader.

Like a female version of Gates, Williamson did her best to keep her followers together and united under their common beliefs and purpose. But the cracks were already starting to show now that local law enforcement had stepped in, and things were compounded by the loss of their founder shortly thereafter. Hoping to produce a new central figure for the Battle Axes, Williamson gave birth on two occasions, but both children were not long for this world and died soon after. They were laid to rest in the hopes of a resurrection that never came, leaving Williamson's idea of bringing a savior into the world unfulfilled. There would be no messiah for the Battle Axes, and their demise was likely hastened even more when a local woman was viciously murdered.

Hannah Shingle (yes, another woman named Hannah) lived just down the road from Free Love Valley and Shenkel Church. Her last name had been Shenkel originally, having morphed over the years for whatever reason into "Shingle." Reports are unclear about whether or not she was or had previously been a member of the Battle Axes, or if she just happened to have the misfortune of living nearby where they had decided to set up shop.

An unmarried woman in her early sixties, Hannah Shingle lived alone. On the fateful day of October 21, 1855, a neighbor of hers came calling at her door, but he received no reply. Immediately worried, he summoned help, and the newly formed posse forced her front door open to enter the farmhouse. There, in the second-floor bedroom, was Hannah Shingle's mutilated body. Blood was everywhere, and her head had been beaten and nearly detached from her body. There was evidence that the intruder had entered her window via a ladder and then wrestled her own hatchet away from her as she attempted to defend herself, turning the weapon upon her to commit the deed.

Although their way of life was fading fast, many of the remaining Battle Axes were immediately suspected of the crime and called in for questioning. And this is where the legends associated with the area of Free Love Valley kick in. One man who was implicated was said to have hanged himself before charges could be brought against him, although whether out of guilt for having committed the murder or just general fear, no one could say. This nameless man has been reported to be seen in the area from time to time. There exists a rumor that another man who was accused of Hannah's murder—but who was never brought to trial—eventually offered a deathbed confession, but there is no proof that such a thing ever occurred. And then of course there is Hannah Shingle herself, whose body rests under a stone that spells her last name as "Shengle" to further confuse matters, but whose spirit may be too restless to depart this world.

Hannah's ghost is not just a modern contrivance, either, since there have been sightings of it dating to just a few years after her murder. Sometimes reported as being headless, and other times with her head still intact, Hannah Shingle is said to roam the short distance of the countryside between her grave at Shenkel Church and the ruins of the farmhouse that was supposedly where she lived and died. Though she doesn't seem to have been of a particularly vengeful nature, one has to wonder if Hannah is searching for her killer. Despite a thorough investigation, no one was ever brought to trial for Hannah Shingle's murder, her death an unsolved mystery that will seemingly remain that way for all time.

Aside from Hannah Shingle perhaps meandering about the area, the church graveyard is regarded as haunted as well. It is said to serve as the final resting place of at least one other murder victim, as well as another pair of individuals who died mysterious deaths. Whatever the case, it is a cemetery out in the countryside, so the creepy vibes will be high no matter what secrets its residents are keeping underground. This particular burying ground originally dates to 1784 and was enlarged shortly after Hannah's burial. Her weathered stone is one of the last ones in the old section of the cemetery, and it is right at the cusp of a downward slope that contains the burials that have taken place in the century and a half since.

Hannah Williamson, for her part, saw the writing on the wall and left Free Love Valley for good about two years after the murder of Hannah Shingle, moving west to seek new converts to her ideology. It is doubtful that she succeeded in her quest, since there is no historical record of her after she abandoned her Battle Axes. Like the sect that she and Gates pushed so fervently, she is a mere footnote of history.

Still, the moniker of "Free Love Valley" has long outlived the cult of folks who inhabited its land over a century and a half ago. It is one of those quirks of local history where people casually use a name for an area while most likely giving very little thought to where it came from. The next time you pass through it or hear its name, take a second to think of just how bizarre it was to have a collective of zealots, free spirits, hippie forerunners, or whatever else you want to call the Battle Axes cavorting about the countryside of Chester County in the middle of the nineteenth century. Just when you think you've heard everything, the events of Free Love Valley remind us that there is always another bizarre chapter of history out there if you dig deep enough.

# Doe Run Village

Location: Routes 82 and 841
39.91592, −75.81772

The Doe Run Village Historic District is along a pleasant, rural stretch of road near the intersection of Routes 82 and 841, and it consists of a smattering of historic buildings that include an old school and church, the ruins of a mill, and even some active residences. A quiet place, but one that produced quite the figure a few centuries ago.

Blacksmith. Soldier. Turncoat. Bandit. Highwayman. Local legend and literary inspiration. This was James Fitzpatrick, a man who ended up at the end of a hangman's noose and had quite the journey to get there. Sorry, I should have warned about that spoiler.

James Fitzpatrick was born in 1748, or thereabouts, and spent his youth in Doe Run Village. Abandoned by his father at an early age, he was apprenticed to a blacksmith and became quite skilled himself. Then, when the struggle for American independence began, Fitzpatrick took up arms and dutifully served his hopeful new country. Until he didn't.

Never one for obeying authority, the dashingly tall, red-haired Fitzpatrick (who also went by the predictable nickname "Fitz" and the slightly more creative "Finch") got himself into trouble with officers on more than one occasion. This led to a flogging, which convinced Fitzpatrick to desert the army and vow "that he would never again wear the blue coat of the army that had rewarded his services by such cruel degradation" (Twaddell 1984, 103). He was captured some time later, imprisoned, and then released when he promised to rejoin his unit. Which, of course, he didn't.

On the verge of being apprehended for a second time, he was able to drive off the soldiers who were sent for him by threatening them with a rifle. It was sometime after this that he went from deserter to full-on seditionist by actively fighting for the British at the Battle of Brandywine, further proving his usefulness by helping to guide the Redcoats through the Chester County landscape that he knew so well. But, true to his restless nature, Fitz did not remain a part of the organized British forces for long, instead taking his crony Mordecai Dougherty and a few other bandits along with him for a countryside tour of robbery and intimidation. Although he was said to be respectful to women and the poor, Fitzpatrick was far from a colonial Robin Hood, with only his own interests at heart.

His main targets were militia officers, tax collectors who were working on behalf of the American cause, and anyone he felt was too supportive of the Continental army. Fitzpatrick, Dougherty, and their crew plundered their fair share of riches, and Fitz also occasionally capped off their activities by beating those whom he had just robbed, subjecting some of them to the whip, or getting more creative. In particular, his treatment of a certain Captain McGowan entered local lore:

> Some he did rob, then let them go free;
> Bold Captain McGowan he tied to a tree.
> Some he did whip and some he did spare;
> He caught Captain McGowan and cut off his hair.

Yes, Fitzpatrick lopped the old-timey ponytail right off the head of Captain McGowan. At least that is as far as he went, though. There is no record of Fitz having killed anyone, except perhaps in battle, although he threatened a great many folks at the end of a gun or sword. Owing to this, some began to think of him as a sort of "gentleman bandit," and a cult following developed. Styling himself as "Captain Fitz," he was already a folk hero of the local loyalists and a thorn in the side of the pesky American rebellion.

Eventually, though, Fitzpatrick's daring crime spree would come to a close in anticlimactic fashion. Fitzpatrick entered the home of Captain Robert McAfee to rob him, but he let his guard down for a moment and McAfee wrestled his pistol away from him. He was subdued, turned over to authorities, and locked away. Despite multiple escape attempts, there was no getting out of this one. James Fitzpatrick was sentenced to hang for his crimes, and that's exactly what happened on September 26, 1778. Sort of.

As you drive down I-95 South through the city of Chester (now in Delaware County, but within Chester County at the time of Fitzpatrick's execution), you go right by the site of his hanging at the corner of Providence and Edgmont Avenues. On that day over 240 years ago, Fitz was strung up to a tree while standing on a cart. The cart was removed from underneath his feet, which should have caused near instantaneous death but didn't, since the rope that was being used was too long. Fitzpatrick's height allowed him to get some of his toes on the ground as he struggled against the inevitable outcome.

In a grotesque scene, the executioner climbed onto Fitzpatrick's back after realizing this, and the added weight caused him to strangle to death after several agonizing minutes. It doesn't get much rougher than that, folks. Some even claimed that the rope used was deliberately made too long, so as to drag out Fitzpatrick's suffering as much as possible as an added punishment for his treachery and blatant disregard for law and order. As a sidenote, his compatriot Mordecai Dougherty was never captured, although some say that he was present at Fitzpatrick's execution and exchanged glances with him to assure Fitz that he would carry on his work.

Although ol' Captain Fitz had shuffled off this mortal coil, he has persisted through the years in a number of ways. First, the legends told about him circulated so greatly and persisted for so long that eventually he was immortalized in fiction. Kennett Square–born author Bayard Taylor strongly based the highwayman character of "Sandy Flash" in his book *The Story of Kennett* (first published in 1866) on Fitzpatrick. In this book the Revolutionary War–era setting is kept, though Sandy Flash's targeted territory switches to what is modern-day Landenberg. As an aside, Taylor led a pretty interesting life himself and has a nifty, barrel-shaped tombstone marking his grave. It is worth checking out at Longwood Cemetery, just off Route 1 in Kennett.

Years after the success of Taylor's work, another book, *Sandy Flash: The Highwayman of Castle Rock*, written in 1922 by Clifton Lisle, further ingrained the legend in the local consciousness. Thus Fitzpatrick became mythologized in a way that few have attained. There are even a couple of streets named "Sandy Flash Drive" in the area, an indirect acknowledgment of his influence. In fact, this is not even the last that we will hear from Fitz in this book, since he will come up during a few discussions in later chapters.

Fitzpatrick's influence may even extend into New Jersey, where some speculate that Tory outlaw Joe Mulliner, the "Robin Hood of the Pine Barrens," had his own legend inflated on the basis of what had already been assigned to Fitzpatrick. Mulliner ended up meeting the same fate, and you can visit his grave in Pleasant Mills, New Jersey. His stone is conveniently etched in large lettering: "THE GRAVE OF JOE MULLINGER HUNG 1781." In case you are wondering, Fitz has no such resting place.

It is said that the ghost of James Fitzpatrick can be seen on horseback, riding throughout Chester County. Maybe he is in search of someone to victimize, or perhaps he is eternally fleeing his would-be captors in an attempt to avoid meeting a grisly end once more. But most believe that the rides of Fitzpatrick are in pursuit of his alleged buried treasure, one that he amassed and then hid somewhere in the rolling hills of Chester County but was unable to retrieve before he was captured and executed.

As far as the reasoning behind ghost stories, the "treasure hunt" angle may be a pretty dubious one. As exciting as it might be to think about gold, silver, and other plunder tucked away somewhere in the local vicinity, this element of the legend is more likely to have been influenced by Bayard Taylor's book, a vestige of the Sandy Flash that he conjured up rather than the actual James Fitzpatrick. Still, if you are in Chester County and see a tall gentleman astride a horse and wearing clothes that look a few hundred years out of date, it would probably be best not to bother him. You wouldn't want a certain Sandy Flash to get any ideas about where your loyalties lie. Just let him pass.

# Devil's Road

Location: Cossart Road, Chadds Ford
39.84738, −75.63403

Cossart Road, better known as Devil's Road, is one of those places you first start to hear about when you are a teenager and easily susceptible to the kind of stories surrounding it—demons, cults, trees that grow in unnatural ways because of the evil presence, etc. It makes for a cool legend, but just what is the deal with this stretch of road that twists its way between Routes 52 and 100 just north of the Delaware border?

For one thing, the basic premise of a lonely road is inherently spooky. The feeling of isolation, off the beaten path, and the uncertainty of what might be lurking in the nearby woods will always be unnerving. Especially if it is dark or you are alone (or both). And there is some legitimate unease along Cossart Road, since the trees that line it do actually peel away from the road. There's a less fun, scientific explanation for this, but many people choose to say this is due to the presence of a building known simply as the "Cult House."

The Cult House has been very difficult for me to pin down, something that is becoming increasingly uncommon in this connected world of ours. I would love to be able to lay eyes on the place or at least figure out exactly where it is located, but I've come up empty. Heck, if you search "Devil's Road Cult House" or "Cossart Road Cult House," you just get a bunch of articles about it and videos of people trespassing or being chased off by other vehicles, but no actual proof of what is happening in this place. I did find out that there was a 2008 film (very) loosely based on the house, called *The House on Devil's Road*, which has a 2.4 score on IMDb. High quality there, obviously. But even that movie also goes by the name *Hell House: The Book of Samiel*, proving that there is zero certainty when it comes to this place. More notably, M. Night Shyamalan's 2004 film *The Village* was inspired both by the woods near Devil's Road and by the Cult House and did much of its filming in the area.

A final Hollywood connection is the 1986 film *At Close Range*, which details the exploits of the infamous Johnston Gang that terrorized Chester County from the 1960s until 1978, when ringleader Bruce Johnston Sr. was apprehended. In a desperate attempt to keep some of his gang members from testifying, Johnston had recently had three of them murdered just off Cossart Road after they were made to dig their own graves. Some say that it was this event that kicked off all the legends of Devil's Road, and that any other tales of satanism and murder were simply heaped on after the fact to add to the lore.

You will find accounts of some people saying that they have seen the house, but curiously there is never much detail to go along with these claims. More frequently, people have stated that they have felt a general unease while driving along Devil's Road, even witnessing strange phenomena such as a flashing blue light. Then, in many cases, they are driven out of the area by dark SUVs that appear out of the woods. Or white vans. Again, sources vary. But either way, sightseeing is most definitely not welcome along Devil's Road.

What we do know, or at least think we know, is that some sort of cult rituals used to go on in this place; hence the name. By whom they were performed we can't say, although many like to point at the du Pont family due to their prominence in the area, figuring that they had to be up to something shady and illicit to consolidate their power and influence. Or maybe it was garden-variety satanists or some hate group fancying itself a religion. The point is, something unnatural and unholy probably went down in the house right along Cossart Road, and the whole area is affected by that energy. Some have even dubbed this general area "Satanville," which doesn't have a local post office but sounds like it could be a great merchandising opportunity for dark tourists.

One twisted legend of the place states that whoever owned the land would take disabled children shortly after they were born and place them in the nearby trees to die. Either that, or they outright sacrificed children among the trees, in keeping with unholy practices. As the trees grew, they would absorb these bodies, some even taking the shape of the child's skull whose life had ended right there. These "skull trees" are also allegedly accompanied by the "Devil's Tree," the roots of which look like a splayed-out hand grabbing at the earth to dig down to hell. A local man even claims that he once saw flames shoot up into the trees and the sound of screaming. Groovy.

Some places just have one story, one ghost, or one moment of history that makes them sufficiently haunted to enter into the collected lore of an area. But Devil's Road is all over the map, with an assortment of things thrown at it in the hopes that enough sticks to deem it adequately haunted for the purposes of legend. In this case it seems that it worked, since most everyone in the area has at least a vague concept of the Devil's Road and Cult House without necessarily knowing many details. Honestly, most regions in the country probably have something similar to fall back on, spinning tales that sound like they were plucked directly from the pages of Alvin Schwartz's *Scary Stories to Tell in the Dark* trilogy.

If you ever scare up the courage to traverse this seemingly sinister road at night in search of the Cult House, good luck to you. You have been warned.

# Fricks Locks Village

Location: 500 Fricks Lock Road, Pottstown
40.22323, −75.59700

The state of Pennsylvania certainly has its fair share of ghost towns. The most famous of these is probably Centralia, the "hell on earth" coal town in Columbia County that was evacuated decades ago due to an underground mine fire that necessitated the destruction and rerouting of a portion of Route 61. This drew oddity seekers from near and far to its abandoned "graffiti highway" until a private company bought the land and buried it under tons of dirt in 2020 for the purposes of reforestation and sending a basic "get off my lawn" vibe to would-be trespassers.

But enough about Centralia; we are here to talk about a ghost town in Chester County—the village of Fricks Locks. Admittedly it's not as cool as Centralia, but we have to embrace the local angle in this odd realm of ghost towns.

Situated near a bend in the Schuylkill River, the area takes its name from John Frick, who originally owned the land but then sold it to the Schuylkill Navigation Company some two centuries ago. A canal was dug and folks set up shop in the area, with a series of locks being built so that ships could safely pass through the area with their cargo. This new Schuylkill Canal was a valuable passageway, especially for the transport of coal, and the village thrived for a time.

Those pesky railroads eventually showed up, though, bleeding the area dry of its main means of supporting itself. It no longer made sense to transport things by ship and be at the mercy of the geography of rivers, and so Fricks Locks became strictly residential and no longer the commerce hub it once was.

As an aside, the area is now officially called "Fricks Locks Historic District." That's fine, but it should really be "Frick's Locks" if the moniker intends to convey that the town is named after John Frick. Or, if it were named after the Frick family as a whole, it would be "Fricks' Locks." In addition, it appears as "Frick's Lock" in Matt Lake's *Weird Pennsylvania*, which has been widely credited with renewing public interest in the area. There were multiple locks in the river alongside the village, so the whole singular/plural thing is particularly confounding. This is a grammaticist's worst nightmare. But I digress.

Fricks Locks, no apostrophes necessary, did ultimately get its own railroad stop and post office (officially designated name: Frick's Lock) in the years to come, but the village was really just on borrowed time until it became a ghost town. The death knell finally started tolling in the 1960s, when PECO decided it was time to construct a nuclear power plant across the river from Fricks Locks, in neighboring Limerick Township. This, owing to federal regulations that no area within about a half-mile radius of such a plant could be inhabited, meant that Fricks Locks was on borrowed time.

Fricks Locks was slowly vacated over the ensuing decades, with residents either being bought out and moving elsewhere or being forcibly evicted off their land, depending on whom you ask about it. Regardless, Fricks Locks was only a collective of boarded-up buildings by the time the power plant started operating in 1986.

As the power plant chugged along, giving the area its very own Simpsons feel, parent company Exelon donated land and structures back to East Coventry Township, which I am sure was done solely out of a sense of charity and preservation and not tax write-offs of any kind. Further money was given to help preserve the area, which now allows the township to benefit from those who wish to pay a fee to see Chester County's own ghost town in person.

Official tours are offered from time to time, although they are historical in nature and do not take guests into the crumbling buildings that might pique the curiosity of many. This doesn't stop Fricks Locks from getting its fair share of looky-loos, however, as large areas of graffiti and vandalism can attest. People just love to check out dilapidated old structures, maybe glimpsing such things as old toilets while they are there. Fun. While it's thrilling, please know that trespassing in Fricks Locks is discouraged, and it is likely to get you a fine at the very least if you are caught.

As for hauntings and the like, there are no main ghost stories surrounding Fricks Locks. John Frick has not been seen sailing along the filled-in canal, searching for someone familiar in the abandoned village that bears his name. That would be a pretty good tale for someone to make up, though. Instead, there has been the usual collection of amateur investigators and ghost-hunting shows that have gone to Fricks Locks to see what they can uncover, coming away mostly with the standard bumps in the night and feelings of general uneasiness. People lived and died there for 150 years, so something at least a little bit eerie was bound to have happened. And if that lends itself to residual energy, well, there you have it.

In the end, this town / village / historic district is a unique piece of Chester County history, a place whose ongoing decay displays the rise and fall of American living in the nineteenth and twentieth centuries. From birth to death, Fricks Locks stands as an unsettling reminder that all things must come to an end. No matter what name you give it.

But wait, there's more.

In 2023, it was announced that the regional planning committee was considering a design for a housing project in the location. The proposal would plop 155 units into a triangular parcel of land, necessitating some changes to the road into Fricks Locks and reviving an area that has remained dormant for decades. It remains to be seen if the plans will be approved or what their ultimate impact could be, but time may be ticking if you hope to get out to Fricks Locks Village and poke around the area before its redevelopment puts an end to the ghost town motif. I guess I never considered that ghost towns could actually die. But apparently it could happen here.

# West Chester: Spook Central?

West Chester, aside from being the county seat of Chester County, really does fit the ideal of a "grand old town." It's dripping with history, going back to its beginnings when it was just "a tavern town called Turks Head" (Mowday 2006, 7). As such, travelers from far and wide stopped in the town, some just passing through, but others staying awhile longer.

The heavy traffic led to a great many businesses and notable buildings going up, making West Chester an underappreciated dream for architecture buffs. The arrival of the university only served to further strengthen its importance and bring it to more prominence. And over the years, general interest in the place has led to more legends and tales of the unexplained per square mile in West Chester than you might otherwise have expected.

We have already discussed the ghost in the clock tower, and further exploration into the former Turk's Head Tavern on North High Street is yet to come. As we mentioned when discussing the clock tower at the old courthouse, local historian Malcolm Johnstone is an authority on the subject of West Chester haunts. His videos posted online by the Chester County Community Foundation, wherein he recounts various stories while clad in old-timey garb, are worth checking out, especially the tale of the red-headed girl on Market Street who was buried alive and now glides around town, seemingly stuck between life and death.

Meanwhile, among the reported ghosts that roam West Chester University's campus is that of former faculty member Dr. G. M. Philips, who was seen on one occasion by New Year's Eve legend Dick Clark, of all people. Other buildings on campus, such as Ramsey Hall and the library, are also said to host their fair share of spirits.

Another popular tale in town concerns a man named John Tully, a horse thief who haunts the edifice that is today known as the Lincoln Building (so named because the first biography of Abraham Lincoln was published in the building in 1860 by Joseph Lewis). In 1788, after Tully was convicted and punished physically with a lashing, he was moved to a cottage located where the Lincoln Building currently sits, 28 West Market Street. Once Tully was there, his moans of pain transformed into laughter, and he literally laughed himself to death overnight.

Tully is said to be buried under the current building; hence his restless spirit roaming about the place, which is today operated by the Chester County Community Foundation. There is a seventeen-minute-long investigative video online if you're into that sort of thing.

Local watering holes such as the Side Bar, Más Cantina, and Iron Hill are also known for spectral activity such as lights turning on and off on their own, unexplained footsteps and clapping, and even the sound of a chain being dragged across the floor. These lively spots appear to be popular among more than just their living clientele.

A few blocks away from the center of town is Everhart Park, also called Everhart Grove, a place where some people have claimed to have had otherworldly experiences. Founded more than a hundred years ago as a place for locals to soak in the nature around them, it remains a quaint strip of land mere blocks from busy residential and commercial areas. It is a nice place to relax in peace and quiet, in theory at least.

On to other matters more generally interesting than spooky: William "Buffalo Bill" Cody saw fit to make West Chester his home for a few years in the 1880s, as strange and out of place as that sounds. No real stories exist about his residence, which still stands at 125 East Washington Street, but it is probably a niftier claim than most towns of this size could boast.

West Chester was even home to the "Invisible Man" himself, actor Claude Rains. Rains first moved to the countryside of Chester County in 1941, before pulling up stakes for the borough of West Chester in either 1956 or 1958, according to differing sources. He lived at the Sharples House (alternately called the Hawthorne House) at 400 South Church Street until leaving the area in 1963, passing away four years later in New Hampshire. Word on the street is that the house was possibly a stop on the Underground Railroad a century before Rains occupied it. Sounds like an opportunity for further study and a commemorative plaque to me. You can still stride by this Greek Revival dwelling today, mere blocks from the university. Rains isn't said to haunt the place or anything, but then again, how would you know if the "Invisible Man" was floating about?

There are "dark history" walking tours of West Chester that are offered from time to time, on which you can learn even more about the borough, and history surrounds you everywhere you turn in this town. This place really does have a lot going on beneath its surface.

# FOUR

## Ghosts and Legends
## at the Inn

When you have centuries of age hanging on you like Chester County does, you are going to have your fair share of inns, taverns, and watering holes that have withstood the test of time and accrued their own lore. Some of these buildings still stand today and operate in such a capacity, while others exist in a preserved form or are utilized for other purposes, and a number have long since bitten the dust, their structural bones bulldozed and their foundations either lying dormant or built upon for something newer and more "useful" to this modern society of ours.

As you will see, the relatively long history of this region has led to an abundance of such places, with no shortage of tales ghostly and otherwise attached to these brick-and-mortar edifices and their nearby areas. We will rely on Meg Twaddell's *Inns, Tales and Taverns of Chester County* a decent bit here, which is decades old but remains a very useful resource for uncovering historical background and firsthand accounts.

As is the case across much of the United States, "public houses" are some of the oldest buildings still standing, because they offered a service to the community and have either continued to do so for generations or became a preserved history site after having fulfilled their original intent. In some cases, historic inns and taverns become something else completely, then are converted back to their roots by enterprising individuals and businesses.

These structures will always have a special aura about them for me and, I suspect, many of the "spookily inclined" folks out there. They are also frequently a welcome respite from the landscape of cookie-cutter strip malls and uninspired construction efforts that our eyes are so accustomed to seeing along the roadside. They're just cool, okay? In this first batch of inns and taverns (more to come later), we look at some of these old and creaky but beautiful places, checking in with employees and patrons alike to uncover some of what may reside within.

Cheers!

# General Warren Inn

Location: 9 Old Lancaster Road, Malvern
40.04274, −75.52453

Whether you spell it "inn" or "inne," the restaurant and the rest of the property at the General Warren predates the founding of our country, having opened in 1745. It has not been in continuous operation since that time, having fallen into disrepair for a long stretch, but today it is thriving in all its colonial glory after it served as an important location amid the American campaign for independence.

We will take our full tour through the vestiges of Chester County's battlefield and war-related haunts in the next chapter, but the General Warren Inn played a role during that time period. It is said that Tories (American colonists loyal to the British Crown) met here following the Battle of Brandywine to help plot the military overture that would become known as the Paoli Massacre, which was either a decisive battle win for the British or an unholy slaughter against unsuspecting colonials, depending on whom you ask to define it.

It makes sense that this would have been the place for such scheming, given that the General Warren Inn sits just over a mile from the site of the Paoli "battle" and was one of the few establishments available for larger gatherings at the time. This is especially true since its owner at the time, a man by the name of Peter Mather, was a known loyalist. Tories would have been hesitant to hold such meetings in their private homes, and they couldn't just meet at a pizza shop, so the Warren was the place. British intelligence officer John André attended meetings and made plans at the General Warren Inn, and it is said that Mather helped supply information about troop movements that led to the Paoli attack.

Precisely because the General Warren Inn acted as the ignition point for such bloodshed, it has been said that the ghosts of massacred colonial soldiers can be seen around the property, either seeking retribution or trying to make their way through some sort of wormhole to prevent the events in Paoli from ever happening. At least one colonial supporter was also tortured for information by the British at this location, with some stories saying the man was a local blacksmith who may have helped supply the final bits of information needed for the Redcoats to pull off the Paoli Massacre. Incidentally, some even say that "Sandy Flash" himself, James Fitzpatrick, was there that fateful evening, helping to guide the British to a sweeping rout of the colonials in a vengeful act against the army that he had deserted.

This place was originally known as "Sign of Admiral Vernon" when it opened in 1745, and it was changed shortly thereafter to "Sign of Admiral Warren." Oddly, this was actually a different Warren (British admiral Sir Peter Warren) than the American patriot Dr. Joseph Warren for whom the tavern was renamed in 1825 and continues to be today, even after much of the original structure burned down in 1831 and was rebuilt in the same fashion. Dr. Warren was mortally wounded at the Battle of Bunker Hill, and he probably tops even Anthony Wayne in terms of the number of places he has lent his name to over the years. This is largely due to his prominence in New England, with the Warren Tavern in Charlestown, Massachusetts, being one such example that is on par with the General Warren Inn of Malvern.

Today this property is simply known as "General Warren," having dropped the "inn" from its name after a rebranding/reimagining a few years ago. At one point I met up with a friend here for happy hour, but it is now a higher-end place, open only for dinner hours and for your very special occasions such as weddings, in addition to offering eight guest rooms as a B&B. So, if you're feeling fancy, you can still make the trek to this historic property to see if you can stir up any echoes of our country's distant past.

# Ship Inn

Location: 693 East Lincoln Highway, Exton
40.03022, −75.61011

D ating to 1796, this building in the middle of a busy commercial area has been able to retain much of its Old World charm. It is now a bustling brewery, VK Brewing Co. & Eatery, which took up residence there in 2022 after the latest incarnation of the Ship Inn restaurant closed. You can slap whatever name you want on a place, but any spirits (nonliquid variety) in the building won't be affected.

Just like the General Warren, the Ship Inn has its roots in the American Revolution and local loyalty to the Crown. The original sign for the Ship Inn, which was located at another site, became target practice for patriot soldiers when the owner, a Tory named Thomas Park, would not serve them. "After this bestowal of the 'patriot's curse' Park's daily trade decreased immensely and he was soon forced to close his doors" (Twaddell 1984, 88). A man named John Bowen bought the bullet-riddled sign and placed it outside his residence, and the current incarnation of the Ship Inn was born. Incidentally, this sign is lost to history, but if anyone comes across an old wooden sign of a painted ship that bears thirteen (an apropos number for colonial times) bullet holes, you may want to scoop it up.

Ghost stories here are generally pretty vague, with former ownership and staff saying that they have felt a presence on the upper floors, which have been less renovated than the common area accessible to the public. An unidentified man, who appears dressed in eighteenth-century attire in accordance with the

inn's earliest days, is the most prominent figure to have been seen. Even though notables such as George Washington and Andrew Jackson are said to have dined at the Ship Inn, there is nothing tying them to this place in the hereafter.

In 2015, the TV program *Ghost Detectives* conducted an investigation of the Ship Inn, with the regular cast joined by members of the Society of Paranormal Research & Education. They spoke to the owners at the time, who described incidents when they heard the sounds of someone running up and down hallways, as well as tables and chairs moving on their own. Investigators captured some of the normal noises and other phenomena that you see during shows of this ilk, but nothing really definitive. They also tried to lure some child ghosts out of the shadows with a jack-in-the-box, which was mildly creepy but didn't result in any payoff.

At one point the investigators leaned a rifle against a door, asking a ghost to take hold of it for protection. A passing mention was made of a murder having occurred there at one time, which was news to me and may have just been a ploy on their part, since I found no record of it in my research. They were able to coax the name of "Thomas" out of a voice box, but their efforts did not reveal anything huge in the end.

The title card at the end of the episode reads "Upon review of all the footage[,] we could not conclude there is paranormal activity at the Ship Inn. However, with past evidence and EVPs (electronic voice phenomena), we don't doubt there is something going on at the Ship Inn. There are still reports of paranormal activity to this day." I am as confused as you are about this contradiction, but I did speak to a few folks at VK Brewing who spend a lot of time in the building, and they confirmed that strange occurrences do occur on a regular basis.

One employee stated that he was rolling silverware late one night with a few other coworkers in one of the side rooms after they had closed for the evening. This particular room was separated from another room by large, cumbersome wooden doors that were closed at the time. Suddenly there was a thunderous noise, and the doors rattled nearly off their hinges. There was not an ongoing storm or other extenuating circumstances. It simply went unexplained. On another occasion a security camera in the bar area caught something odd. The bar was decorated with some lighted garland for the holiday season, which seemed to pull itself down from its anchors without warning, sending the attached lights crashing to the floor. Happenings such as these have led to VK brewing up a beer called "Haunted Haze," a New England IPA whose can features the building set against a full moon.

Even if you are skeptical about the disturbances at the historic Ship Inn building, you can still come for an aura of history, a beer, and a couple of bites of food. It won't be an exact re-creation of the sumptuous feasts that supposedly occurred at the Ship Inn with regularity in years past, but you will be standing on history. And that always brings a bit of an interesting flair to an otherwise average day.

# Stottsville Inn

Location: 3512 Strasburg Road, Coatesville
39.95977, −75.88819

There exist some places in Chester County where you forget about the area's rural roots, locales where it is easy to get swept up among the crowds, and they seem as busy and energetic as a pocket of a large city like Philadelphia. A place that seems to find you and swallows you up during your time there.

The Stottsville Inn is definitely not one of those places.

Located at the base of an odd, Y-shaped intersection in an area that can be generously referred to as "the sticks," this hotel/restaurant/bar has been a staple of the area since 1858. Happily, it has been restored in recent years to its former glory after looking like it wasn't long for this world.

Under previous management, one of the signature offerings on the menu was a dish named "Chicken Josephine." It was named after the resident spirit at the place, a woman named Josephine Chandler, who was said to have lived on the property many years ago before "she was murdered by her lover, a man named Horace" (Adams 2001, 158). Stricken with guilt, Horace then supposedly offed himself by getting a cow to kick him in the head. Okay then. At any rate, Josephine was said to sit and wait for her lover for years afterward in the dining room, apparently unaware that they had both crossed over.

That's one story.

Another version of the tale says that "he [Horace] murdered her because he came home and found her in this room in bed with another man. So Horace choked her lover, Chadwin Martin, and Josephine to death" (D'Angelo 2008). As a result, Martin's ghost now roams about on the second floor, stirring up the usual kind of poltergeist activity you would expect. Meanwhile, "Josephine tends to lurk through the entire building and she is very unpredictable. She displays her presence by turning on and off the lights and water, and knocking over wine bottles" (D'Angelo 2008). Her spirit was felt largely by the owners and staff for years, and they just dealt with it.

In 2007 and 2008, some very thorough investigations were conducted here by multiple researchers who came armed to the teeth with a bevy of equipment. Their main target was the room in which Josephine had been murdered, room 305. Supposedly their equipment sensed major temperature fluctuations in the room, in concurrence with the belief that cold spots are strong indicators of residual spirit activity. The investigators also captured a voice on their recorder that said, "I want to leave immediately!"

Moving out of room 305, more cold spots were discovered throughout the Stottsville Inn, and moving shadows were captured on camera in a number of locations. Playing back the camera recordings also led investigators to discover a shaking phenomenon, as though something nearby was disturbing the cameras and causing them to vibrate, even though they were set up in empty rooms and hallways. There were tapping noises heard at several points of the investigation, and one of the ghost hunters said he felt a pushing sensation against his body. Researchers came away from the experience reporting general feelings of uneasiness and a strong belief that there were multiple active presences in the building.

Disappointingly, the Stottsville Inn website doesn't say anything about its colorful past, making only the usual generic statements about it being "an authentic piece of Chester County history" and the like. I suppose that owners of any historic property always have to weigh the pros and cons of openly discussing such things, and in this particular case they have decided not to play up the whole paranormal angle for public consumption. But talk to staff and you will get an inkling of the kinds of unseen guests that still take up residence at the Stottsville Inn, both on the upper floors where Josephine allegedly met her fate as well as in the basement and kitchen. It is enough to drive the curious to go check it out for a meal or—if they dare—book a room and stay on the premises to see whom or what they might run into.

# Letty's Tavern

Location: 201 East State Street, Kennett Square
39.84733, −75.71046

There is definitely something going on at Letty's Tavern, located along the lively main drag of Kennett Square. And I don't just mean brunch.

This distinctive-looking building situated in the heart of downtown Kennett at the corner of North Broad and East State Streets was built in 1835. It originally served as a private residence, which the owners expanded over subsequent years. As is the case with these old buildings, it was repurposed later on, and it eventually became known as the "Green Gate Tea Room" in 1927. This was during Prohibition, of course, with no alcohol allowed to be peddled on the premises (although that doesn't mean it didn't happen). Once Prohibition ended a few years later, the structure went into full-on tavern mode.

In 1976 the place was christened the Kennett Square Inn, and ghostly encounters took off. For whatever reason, probably just in a nod to the historical significance of the general area, most of the odd activity was attributed to the spirit of a girl named Letitia, which was the name of William Penn's daughter. In fact, the area now known as Kennett Square had once been part of a tract of land named "Letitia's Manor" after Penn had granted thousands of acres to her back in the day. So it made at least some degree of sense to run with the Letitia angle. Whether it is just a cutesy naming convention for the spirit girl or a supposition that Letitia Penn is the presence on hand at the inn, people can decide on their own.

The spectral activity was wild. A chef reported that things would fall off shelves and then spin around unnaturally after landing on the floor. And a former owner of the Kennett Square Inn said that he had a waking nightmare of sorts, where a cold darkness rolled into his room and then he experienced a jostling sensation like a child was jumping up and down on his bed, as youngsters are apt to do.

Customers had ghostly visions as well. One woman enjoying dinner at the establishment reported that after her husband left the table to go to the bathroom, a young girl around age thirteen and dressed in very old-fashioned clothing appeared in his seat. This girl then disappeared just as quickly as she had arrived, leaving the woman wondering what had just happened.

Another former owner of the place once was awakened in the middle of the night by a phone call from local police. It seemed that a call had come into the police station from the pay phone inside the Kennett Square Inn, even though the whole building was locked and nothing was found when the owner and the police went to check it out.

Of course, as you've probably discerned, this building's current name, "Letty's Tavern," is an abbreviated and affectionate reference to Letitia Penn, its supposed resident spirit (or at least the naming inspiration for it). The naming decision was made by the new owners when, as they were hanging wallpaper and renovating in preparation for the opening of the restaurant, they heard unmistakable footsteps and running sounds on the floors above them. Given the previous reputation of the building, they figured that Letitia was still there, and named it in her honor.

No, Letitia Penn never actually set foot in this building, and she hadn't even been in Pennsylvania for many years by the time she died in England in 1745. But she makes for the best "jumping-off point" here to give this ghost story a historical connection.

When I first became aware of the Kennett Square Inn several years ago, I wanted to grab a meal there and enjoy some of the historical vibes. But I was told, "Don't bother; you're not missing anything." The place apparently was so stuffy and outdated that it still boasted one of the few cigarette machines around. I like old stuff, but not in that way. And so I never set foot inside the building until after it was renovated and became Letty's Tavern in 2021.

I was able to explore this one (okay, by "explore" I mean that I went in for a drink) and get some information straight from the horse's mouth when I visited for the first time in late 2022. When I asked a couple of members of the staff if they had ever had any strange experiences, I was answered in the affirmative. The bartender pointed out the wooden shelves at the bar, which displayed all of their liquor bottles. The shelves used to be glass, until staff came in one morning only to find them completely smashed. And while it is true that big trucks regularly rumble along the narrow street right in front of the building, it seems as though it would have taken an excessive amount of vibration to knock over multiple shelves tucked pretty far inside the entrance. Another time, a few of the tavern's regular patrons watched a glass fall off the shelf on its own and shatter right before them. No word on how many drinks they may have already consumed at that point of the evening, though.

Other experiences of note include the staff hearing excessive footsteps on the main floor above them while they were going through inventory in the bottle shop downstairs, a space that is today occupied by the Tired Hands Brewing Company Taproom. The restaurant was closed and otherwise unoccupied at the time, but the sounds from above were unmistakable. To go along with this, a female staff member also told me that she and others distinctly heard a baby's cry, which they swore was from inside the building. Their search came up empty but, just to be sure, someone quickly went outside to see if anyone was nearby. There were no babies in sight. So make of that what you will.

Whether it is Letty herself, some other spirit, or a collection of former folks who are somehow stuck in this Kennett Square building, Letty's Tavern is a worthy waypoint for residents and travelers to get some good food and a drink and maybe see or hear something interesting as a bonus part of the experience.

# Inn at St. Peter's Village

Location: 3471 St. Peter's Road, St. Peter's
40.17801, −75.73099

T he small village of St. Peter's, formerly known as the village of French Creek Falls, has "quaint" written all over it. Strolling along its streets is virtually guaranteed to take you back to the late 1800s, the time period during which the Inn at St. Peter's Village was built stone by stone and was originally dubbed the Excursion House during the town's heyday as a mining hub for black granite.

The inn is a downright charming place, but even with the passage of time, some guests have never checked out. As is par for the course, we have had the slamming of many doors over the years at the inn, and former workers have mentioned lights popping on for no reason. One specific spook is that of a woman, apparently despondent with grief, who committed suicide at the inn many years ago for reasons that have been lost to history. This unfortunate lady mills about the dining room from time to time. Another female ghost has been spotted looking out over French Creek, which runs behind the hotel and offers a picturesque backdrop to the area. True to form, this lady also disappears before the beholder can make heads or tails of the situation. A local shopkeeper and lifelong resident of "the village" told me that he has seen the figure of a lady on the balcony of the inn, looking out over St. Peter's Road on many occasions, as if she's taking stock of the goings-on in town.

Also without rhyme or reason, the sound of a crying child has been recorded in reports as far back as the 1940s by employees and hotel guests alike. No one has ever found the source of these cries. But before you start getting too creeped out over disembodied babies, allow me to introduce you to a more benevolent ghost that haunts the Inn at St. Peter's Village—Herbie.

Herbie is said to be the spirit of local baker Herb Hinkle, a very nice man who for one reason or another stuck around after departing this mortal coil. It is said that years ago, workers at the hotel watched with wide eyes as doors opened on their own, their ears perked up at the sound of loud, unexplained footsteps, and the hairs stood up on the backs of their necks as a result of feeling someone being right over their shoulders. All of this was attributed to the dearly departed Herbie. But that's as far as it went, since Herbie wouldn't do anything harmful to anyone; he just wants to make his presence known.

It is not just the old hotel and restaurant building but the entire village itself and the surrounding French Creek valley that seems to have a "trapped in the past" aura just hanging over it. Singing, walking ghosts have been seen and heard along the creek and around town, with some of these sightings

being ascribed to the spirit of "Aunt Lena," a former resident. But the best bit of local lore doesn't even seem to involve spectral activity, instead telling the tale of a rather clever counterfeiter and horse thief who faked his own death to elude his pursuers:

> He somehow arranged for everything to fall in place and summoned a doctor, a minister, an undertaker, and gravediggers to fake his death and burial. Perhaps paying them in his bogus bills, the chap managed to pull it off. He could certainly not be arrested if he was buried six feet under. What's more, by the time, if ever, the authorities got wise to his ruse, he'd be long gone and far away (Adams 2001, 91).

That turned out be the case, since police dug up his grave only to find a big bag of sand, and the bandit was never apprehended. So here we have a case of at least one person escaping St. Peter's Village rather than being stuck there for eternity.

The next time you are looking for somewhere peaceful and bucolic to visit, even if just for an hour or two, you should consider the village of St. Peter's and its iconic inn. Because if it is good enough for the departed to stick around for decades, it's good enough for you in your corporeal form.

# Red Rose Inn

Location: 804 West Baltimore Pike, West Grove
39.82420, −75.87003

S itting mere feet from an entirely too-busy intersection (trust me, I go through there all the time) in the area known as Jennersville, the Red Rose Inn does a good job of hiding an interesting history.

It's a sturdy, ordinary-looking brick structure with an unassuming—I'll go as far as to call it boring—sign hanging from the front porch that proclaims its name, and you probably wouldn't guess that the building is more than two hundred years old. Yes, there have been extensive overhauls, but the point stands.

Here is its history in brief, courtesy of Penn Township's website:

> The origin of the Inn dates back to the 1700s when 5,000 acres was deeded to William Penn, III. The property was leased at a cost of one red rose per year. The deed specifically stating, "his heirs and assigns forever pay one Red Rose, on the 24th day of June, if same be demanded." Thus how the name "Red Rose Inn" eventually came about. In 1742 William Penn deeded the 5,000 acres to his grandson, William Allen. Allen sold about 55 of the 5,000 acres to a Samuel Cross in 1748. The original structure of the Red Rose Inn, which is that structure that is still standing today, had allegedly already been built by Cross between 1731 and 1740.

The inn was sold, renovated, resold, and rerenovated numerous times over the ensuing decades, and it even functioned as a place to board employees of the National Fireworks Company during World War II. For many years it served locals as a bar and restaurant, and it is said to have been a frequent hangout of the infamous Johnston Gang during their various crime sprees. And through virtually all of its existence, the Red Rose Inn has been quite haunted.

From a "haunted horseman" who is said to trot nearby, to the ghost of a young girl who met a violent end, to a Native American dubbed (in a very un-PC fashion) "Indian Joe," the Red Rose may have more individual entities than any of the other single structures in the county that we have discussed.

As for Joe, his sad tale is the most interesting one bandied about the place. Legend says that the innkeeper's young daughter, Emily, was murdered. Locals were suspicious of anyone whom they deemed to be an outsider, and they set their sights on Joe, since he was seen nearby just before the heinous act occurred. Adams explains, "Although evidence pointed away from him as the killer, he was convicted in a kangaroo court, hanged on the property, and buried in the dirt basement of the oldest part of the inn. After his lynching the identity of the actual murderer was discovered. But it was too late for Joe" (Adams 2001, 82). As a result, Joe's tortured spirit refuses to remain silent, and he is said to wander about the place for eternity. The fate of the true killer, a local drunk who stumbled into the woods and passed out after committing the deed, is lost to history.

It is reported that years ago, calculators in the office began flying off the desk. Remember calculators? You can tell that an anecdote is dated when they get mentioned. There have also been recorded instances of doors slamming on their own, and a mirror being smashed to bits. And Emily herself, the poor murdered girl, has turned up a time or two. The former proprietor reported watching TV in bed late one evening when his door was pushed slowly and creepily ajar. There, standing in a fine dress and cuddling a doll, was Emily. And then she was gone.

Other disturbances include electronics turning off on their own, as well as sheets being pulled off beds. An unidentified female ghost even appeared at the bar after closing time one night, ordered a drink, and then vanished right before the bartender's eyes.

Some decades ago, the Red Rose's owners opened their doors to researchers from Temple University, who declared "that they could feel the presence of two spirits within the house: a male, whose musky scent brought about the image of an Indian, and a young girl who emanated a light, airy fragrance" (Twaddell 1984, 154). Joe and Emily just knocking about, I suppose. The same owner also says that a short while after this investigation, she was giving a tour to dinner guests when a wineglass was forcefully smacked out of her hand by an unseen entity and shattered when it hit the floor. Upon returning to the room to clean up the scattered broken glass, she discovered that it was in a tidy pile, ready for easy disposal.

Nowadays the Red Rose Inn no longer functions in its longtime capacity,

but it is looked after by Penn Township, which opens the doors on a quarterly basis for a public "open house." You can tread the boards, learn even more about the history of the property, and perhaps even annoy the guides with questions about ghosts and legends. I highly recommend it.

# FIVE

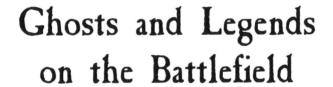

## Ghosts and Legends
## on the Battlefield

The entire state of Pennsylvania played a major role in the struggle for independence and the American Revolution. No surprise there, since Philadelphia was HQ for our nascent nation. But a few miles west of the city, Chester County was home to several major events that transpired in 1777 and 1778. For this section, it makes sense to go through things chronologically, since the outcome of one event ostensibly led to the next. War doesn't exactly follow a set schedule.

You will find no vestiges of Civil War battles or skirmishes in Chester County, since the fighting never made its way here. Instead, you will need to take a short trip west to places such as Gettysburg to transport yourself to that point in time. And so we are staying colonial in this chapter, as we follow the Continental forces and their enemy combatants through a normally idyllic Chester County that saw its share of violence, suffering, and death over just a few short months during the American Revolution.

These spots harken to a vital epoch in American history, which is underselling things, because we would not even have the United States of America without the events that transpired during this period of time.

# Brandywine Battlefield

Location: 1491 Baltimore Pike, Chadds Ford
39.87455, −75.57627

It is difficult to pin down Brandywine Battlefield, but we will give it our best shot, since the battle that took place between the Continental army (Americans) and the bad guys (British) here in September 1777 was a pretty big deal.

The visitor center (*see address*) and the main park are in Delaware County, but of course the battle was not confined to one location. Many important places and markers associated with it are found on the other side of the Brandywine in Chester County, and so we can discuss the battlefield and the battle itself without feeling as if we are cheating too much on the concept of this book.

As part of their defense of Philadelphia against the British, the fledgling American army set up shop in Chadds Ford, in accordance with the age-old military tenet of "defending the high ground." Under General George Washington the rebels were ready for an assault by the British, but they were swarmed on the afternoon of September 11, 1777, and were unable to beat back the attack in heavy fog, which spanned across an incredibly large swath of land (over 10 square miles) that you can take scenic driving tours of or explore on foot today.

All told, this ended up being the largest battle of the war. It was a big victory for the British, although the Continental army had shown well enough to keep their morale high, since they were able to live to fight another day despite being pushed out of the area. The rest of this chapter will follow the action in chronological order after this point. As for the vestiges of the past, there are many that reside in and around the Brandywine Battlefield.

Spirits have purportedly been seen near the peace garden, which is between the Birmingham-Lafayette Cemetery and the Birmingham Friends Meetinghouse. This cemetery contains a common grave of British and American soldiers, and foggy weather reminiscent of the battle conditions of September 11, 1777, is said to bring out ghost sightings in the area. Some historical reenactors have even claimed seeing phantom soldiers in costume who look the part and then fade away during the festivities. Apparitions of horses have been spotted as well, vanishing when observers get too close to them.

There have also been reports of general fighting sounds, such as musket and cannon fire and the yelling and screaming of troops in the heat of battle. One ghost walking about the area is particularly notable because his feet are not visible, as though he were moving at a ground level below what currently exists. This makes sense, because some of the landscape was lower at the time of the battle and has been built up in the centuries since. Overall, it appears that soldiers from both sides never rest as they honor their oath to fight for their cause.

Thornbury Farm (1256 Thornbury Road in West Chester) is a few miles from the visitor center, but it also carries importance here. Now a venue for weddings and other events, Thornbury Farm also features private ghost classes and guided tours where you can come out and possibly rub elbows with the ghosts of the past. And that's because this farm ended up being the site of the final troop engagement of the battle, during which Americans became trapped between encroaching British and Hessian soldiers. According to Thornbury Farm's website:

> So many Americans were shot and bayonetted, it was said the blood flowed over two miles to the Brandywine. The barn and large deep spring house were used to hold prisoners and the main house was used as a hospital. During the gruesome surgery practices of that time, limbs of hurt soldiers were thrown out the window. Two mass burial sites on the property were used to dispose of the dead.

This of course has prompted several investigations by mediums and paranormal groups over the years, most notably a trip from *Ghost Hunters* in 2009. The various probes of the property have supposedly revealed as many as nine distinct spirits, such as the former owner of the farm who hanged himself, a crying young girl, and a man who froze to death. This place is apparently a hotbed of colonial-era activity.

Chadds Ford Inn (now Brandywine Prime steak house along Route 1) is just outside the Chester County line. And so, while we can't dedicate an entire section to it for our purposes, it should be known that the property is said to host a pair of child ghosts who go by the names Katie and Simon. The newest owners have not reported any unusual activity over the past few years, however. The inn and its surrounding area were overrun by the British after the Battle of Brandywine, which may or may not have had a hand in any future spectral happenings.

Not only did the Battle of Brandywine produce a number of legends in the immediate area, but its fallout extended into the town of West Chester and to the Turk's Head Tavern, which we will discuss later in the book. Thanks to the pivotal role that this battle played in our country's fight for independence, the whole area is today nicely preserved as an important reminder of our nation's origins and the echoes of the past that still visit us on this earthly plane even after centuries have elapsed.

# Battle of the Clouds

Location: 133 Phoenixville Pike, Malvern
40.04213, −75.57762

Well, this one was a dud. In fairness, though, sequels are hard. Following a valiant defeat at the Battle of Brandywine, American troops were on the run. A few days later, on September 16, 1777, they prepared to meet the British in their next engagement near Malvern, but inclement weather threw a wrench into things. Today, if you are in the area visiting the site of the Paoli Massacre and Duffy's Cut, you might as well swing by the historical marker for this aborted battle. It is at the coordinates above in front of the former White Horse Tavern, which is today a private residence, and it reads:

### BATTLE OF THE CLOUDS

Following the September 1777 Battle of Brandywine, Continental forces retreated to regroup along Swedesford Road near the White Horse Tavern. With British troops in pursuit, the onset of a sudden downpour and resulting wet gunpowder delayed an imminent confrontation. Outnumbered Continental forces were able to retreat northwest, securing fresh supplies and ammunition. A loss here would have been disastrous to the American cause.

So it stands to reason that this seemingly forgettable incident in American history was an absolutely pivotal one to the concept of "America" in general. We very well may not have won the war and become a country if not for the rainout that saved the colonists' bacon on that day. Divine providence, random chance, or something else? You be the judge. There is also an older plaque commemorating the "battle" next to Villa Maria Hall on the Immaculata University campus a few miles south.

The encounter was not a total washout, with a few dozen casualties reported, but the daylong deluge quickly moved in and prevented things from getting any fiercer and bloodier. With both armies unable to advance through the muck, General Washington retreated to plan for another day.

Unfortunately, the aborted battle at Malvern played into the British scheming to pull off the "Paoli massacre" sneak attack that we will discuss next. But the delay of a full-scale engagement on September 16, 1777, ultimately helped keep the struggling Continental army intact long enough to get through the next few months and the winter encampment at Valley Forge before rallying to turn the tide of the war over the next four years.

And that is essentially the story here. Troops on both sides did indeed die on this spot, and the "Battle of the Clouds Park," which is about a quarter mile up the road from the historical marker, is now an open area containing sports fields and a playground. It is also neighbored by a couple of cemeteries, including Haym Salomon Memorial Park, where you can drop in and say hello to singer/songwriter Jim Croce. Sorry to disappoint you, but there are not any ghost stories or other folklore to dig into here, just a cool bit of underappreciated American history.

# The Paoli Massacre

Location: Near Monument and Wayne Avenues, Malvern
40.02958, −75.51917

Following the loss at Brandywine and the nonstarter of "the Battle of the Clouds," American forces found themselves in the Paoli/Malvern area as they continued in their endeavors to defend Philadelphia despite pushback from the British. This site is where the ruthless attack and ambush took place that resulted in another bloody day for our nation.

Today, Paoli Battlefield Historical Park is a serene, wide-open space highlighted by the obelisk situated at the crest of the looping road that enters the area. It also features numerous markers, informational plaques, and pieces of artillery dotting the wooded area, which can quite literally take you on a step-by-step tour of what occurred the night of September 20, 1777.

Important events occurred at nearby Warren Tavern, as we have previously discussed. For the purposes of the battle itself, we first need to know that our pal General Anthony Wayne led this particular group of ill-fated Continental soldiers who fell victim to the attack after 10 p.m. As the Americans slept, British soldiers quietly unloaded their muskets, fixed their bayonets, and stealthily maneuvered into position. True to the moniker of a "massacre," the surprised Americans never really stood a chance at a proper battle.

The most-accurate accounts given say that 272 American troops were either killed or captured as a result of the entanglement, with hardly any British casualties at all. General Wayne, who seemingly failed to recognize how much danger his men were in, was later charged with misconduct but was ultimately acquitted of any wrongdoing or negligence. This is despite it being strongly suggested that he escaped death that evening only by "turning his uniform coat inside out to display its red lining, passing himself off as a British officer. Thus we find the origin of the word turncoat in the English language" (Twaddell 1984, 29). Very interesting if true, but of course Wayne denounced such slander to his reputation, and the courts agreed with him.

One specific spirit said to haunt the area for eternity is the so-called Guilty Ghost of Paoli, an American soldier who lived locally and had received special permission to spend the night at home once his work at camp was done. As the tale goes, this unnamed soldier had a nightmare about his encampment being attacked one evening, which is where Charles J. Adams III (2001) picks up in *Ghost Stories of Chester County and the Brandywine Valley*:

> He managed to shake off the nightmare, roll over, and go back to sleep. But within minutes, the vision came back to him. In a sweaty panic, he leapt out of bed, hurriedly put on his uniform and, despite his wife's protestations, mounted his white horse and galloped back to camp. With campfires casting an eerie glow on the grounds, he looked across his camp with horror. All he could see was battered, beaten, and bruised men. All he could hear were the moaning, groaning sounds of agony. All he could smell was the stench of death. At once, he heard a rustling sound. It was a British soldier, running from the nearby underbrush. The Colonial trooper jerked around and looked up to see his adversary's sword gleaming in the moonlight. The sword came down in a frightful blur, taking the young American's head with it! (p. 26)

This probably apocryphal tale of the final casualty of the Paoli Massacre has real *Sleepy Hollow* vibes, but it has persisted over the years. Some say that this now-headless horseman rides his mount to and fro across the battleground, looking for a chance to turn his weapon on someone even in death, since he never had the opportunity before his fateful end. The night of the battle, September 20, would seem to be the best time to catch a glimpse of the guilty ghost, but he supposedly has shown up on other occasions.

The original Paoli monument, erected in 1817, still exists at the park, although the impressive main obelisk was constructed to replace it in 1877. It stands guard over a mass grave that contains fifty-three of the American soldiers who were brutally attacked and slain one hundred years earlier. One side of the stone reads:

HERE REPOSE THE REMAINS

OF FIFTY THREE

AMERICAN SOLDIERS

WHO WERE THE VICTIMS OF

COLD BLOODED CRUELTY

IN THE WELL KNOWN

MASSACRE AT PAOLI

WHILE UNDER THE COMMAND OF

GENL. ANTHONY WAYNE

AN OFFICER WHOSE MILITARY CONDUCT

BRAVERY AND HUMANITY

WERE EQUALLY CONSPICUOUS THROUGHOUT

THE REVOLUTIONARY WAR.

Aside from the unnecessary shout-out to Wayne, it is important to note that the term *massacre* holds sway here, since the military ideal of a fair and legitimate battle was not met. The verbiage strongly suggests a war crime, and Paoli really did act as a rallying cry for the American cause as news spread of what had transpired that evening. The "guilty ghost" and dozens of other supposed spirits of soldiers that have been felt over the decades only serve to enhance the legend of the area and make sure that we do not forget an important piece of our history.

Today, the Paoli Battlefield Preservation Fund offers paranormal tours to help satiate public curiosity about the area, and you can get the inside scoop about the mass burial site and encounters that have been had in the area over the years. For the sake of our local and national history, we should all "Remember Paoli."

# Valley Forge

Location: 1400 North Outer Line Drive, King of Prussia
40.10150, −75.42296

Right off the bat, I will acknowledge that I am somewhat cheating again by grouping Valley Forge along with the other sites that hosted actual engagements between military combatants. But the encampment of George Washington and his troops at Valley Forge does not occur without said battles, and so it fits here on a technicality. Also, the majority of the park is in Montgomery County, including the visitor center, which is the address given. Nevertheless, this is important to the area since it was a result of the battles that were fought in Chester County, so let's run with it.

You could fill a small library with all the literary works that have been penned about the Continental army's encampment under General Washington during the winter of 1777–78, so I won't bother revisiting information that you can access much more completely elsewhere. Basically, when it comes to residual energies and tales of lore that exist around Valley Forge today, you can chalk it all up to the fact that it was the site of so much misery, as American troops died from disease in large numbers during the harsh winter spent there while they licked their wounds and attempted to regroup (successfully, it turned out) for the battles yet to come. Stories are all over the place, and here is a sampling, beginning with an 1895 report from the Philadelphia Press, as re-counted by D. P. Roseberry (2007):

> It is said that the spirits of the dead Revolutionary soldiers flit along the hillsides on stormy nights and visit the shadowy spots where they once gathered around the camp fire and that ghostly campfires have been seen flickering among the trees on starless nights and the faint echo of a challenge and countersign could be heard from the lips of spirit sentinels (p. 121).

An old-timey recollection about an even old-timier time, which is always fun. It is all pretty eerie and unsettling, since when you visit the park, you basically find yourself walking in the very spots where so many soldiers suffered and died. The spook show also reportedly continues at the Isaac Potts House, the building that functioned as General Washington's headquarters during the encampment. One reported story says that a park guide was changing into period-era clothing for work inside the building when he suddenly felt someone behind him adjusting his coat, like a tailor would during a fitting. He thought it was a coworker, but the room was empty when he turned to face them. A man hanging from a tree in the woods has also been sighted near Washington's headquarters. Legend says that he was a spy who was executed at that exact spot, his unsettled spirit now confined to the place where he met his violent end.

Just like at Brandywine Battlefield, people report seeing men in tattered military uniforms, assuming them to be part of a reenactment, only for these soldiers to vanish into thin air. One history teacher in the 1970s even went so far as to recount a tale where he was taken at bayonet point by one of these "reenactors" to a senior officer, who questioned the teacher about what he was doing there. It was only after the teacher got fed up enough with the situation and told them that the war was over and he didn't wish to partake in this role play any longer that the officer ordered the soldier to return the man to where he found him. After heading back to where he had been taken in the first place, the teacher turned to find the soldier suddenly gone. Had he really encountered a pair of spirits who believed that they were still fighting their war?

Our friend the esteemed General Wayne is commemorated by a large statue at Valley Forge, and it is said that the head of the statue rotates when the full moon is out. Does this have something to do with his spirit rising from its grave to resume its ride to collect its missing bones? Nobody knows, but it would be a cool way to tie the legend together.

There is also a pseudo-cryptid that lurks about the area, the not-so-famous "Cat Man." It is said that many years ago, a local man had a peculiar fixation with cats, so much so that he would let his fingernails grow very long so that he could partake of canned cat food by scooping it out of its tin with his nails. Gross. Further, this man apparently became very despondent that he could not grow his own tail to complete the feline conversion, so he took it upon himself to rip off the tail of any cat that crossed his path, black or otherwise. Locals claimed to see empty cans lying about the area, fueling further speculation of the Cat Man, but there were never any reports of him attacking anyone or otherwise haunting the area after he faded from memory.

Another legend says that there are unmarked graves of American soldiers along Route 23, the modern road that runs right near the visitor center, Washington Memorial Chapel, and several of the monuments at Valley Forge. But this has largely been debunked, since any bones found underground in this area almost certainly belong to animals that were in camp with the soldiers and who either died from illness or were slaughtered for food.

Other tales are told about Valley Forge that are unrelated to the soldiers who struggled to exist during the harsh months spent there. The ghost of a child, said to be the otherworldly remnants of a youngster struck and killed by a car in the 1950s, has been spotted at dusk near the roadway. A man carrying a lantern, seemingly attempting to get the attention of passing motorists for an undetermined reason, has surfaced from time to time as well. And the old, abandoned Port Kennedy Railroad Station, located near the park, has also been cited as a hotspot for spectral activity over the years.

Anyone interested in further paranormal studies of Valley Forge is in luck, since there are a multitude of videos and photos from its many investigations that can be found online. The history and the mystique surrounding this area are undeniable, and it won't be going away for as long as the United States is in business.

# Phoenixville: A Rebuttal to West Chester

As discussed, the borough of West Chester is positively oozing with the kinds of history, tales, and legends that get folks interested in learning more about the place and subsequently either settling down there or at least visiting frequently and injecting dollars into local coffers. But West Chester has some company in Chester County, since Phoenixville has sprung to life over the last few decades, asserting itself as being worthy of just as much attention.

We have discussed its library and all the stories surrounding it, but a number of other buildings in town carry some weight as well. One such place is on South Whitehorse Road, where there currently exists a consignment shop that was a restaurant a few years ago. Before that it was a private home where a thirteen-year-old girl who lived there tragically fell down the stairs and died. Former staff members reported a pushing feeling anytime that they went by the girl's old bedroom, and there have been other cases of items being moved off tables on their own and a cigar smell permeating the air when the building was unoccupied.

The former Fountain Inn on Nutt Road, which is a pizza joint as of this writing, was once ransacked by British troops during the Revolution. Unfortunately for those Redcoats, a local farmer had hidden his beehives in the building to protect them, and said bees attacked the marauding soldiers when their hives were discovered. As such, it is said that the apparition of a terrified soldier can be seen in the corner of the basement of the old Fountain Inn. This edifice and others around town are part of a regular walking tour that occurs during the Halloween season, as guests can experience "the most haunted borough in Pennsylvania," according to Phoenixville denizens.

When it comes to Phoenixville folklore, I will say that I was supremely disappointed by the Colonial Theatre (yes, they use the fancy English spelling) when I dug into it. Don't get me wrong, I have been to the Colonial several times, and it's a fantastic venue. But you would think that such a building would have accumulated some good tales over the course of one hundred years. And yet, nothing out of the ordinary seems to have occurred there in all that time.

Aside from the countless ghosts and ghouls that have graced its silver screen, there are no real records of anything unusual going bump in the night at the Colonial. Film projectors shutting off on their own? Strange whispers from the balcony? Haunted Goobers at the concession stand? You name it, and it hasn't happened.

Yes, they famously shot some of *The Blob* at the Colonial in the 1950s, but the film was as hokey as it was scary, leaving no residual aura of a "cursed film" or anything moderately creepy for the public to glom on to. So, while the Colonial's annual BlobFest is really cool and they have a nice display case in the lobby, there isn't much else to speak of, not even any reports of a phantom usher sweeping up popcorn. It's a real bummer. The more interesting morsel of history surrounding *The Blob* concerns the fact that it was produced by Good News Productions (GNP), a local film company in nearby Yellow Springs, about 7 miles away from the Colonial. GNP dealt almost exclusively in religious films, TV, and radio that espoused a Christian message, but *The Blob* was a rare foray into the mainstream for them. They tapped the Colonial as the site for the movie's showcase scene, eventually sold the film to Paramount, and movie history was made.

GNP later made another sci-fi film, *4D Man*, to much less acclaim. GNP lasted from 1952 to 1974, and today it is commemorated by a historical marker at the corner of Art School Road and Yellow Springs Road. Also of note, the Chester Springs Soldiers' Orphans School operated at this site from 1868 until 1912, providing education and care for children who had lost their parents, or whose families were otherwise destitute. Sadly, it is reported that twenty-one of these young boys and girls died at the school during this time period and had nobody to claim their bodies. They all are buried under a memorial marker at Vincent Baptist Meeting House, some 2 miles away. This wasn't in Phoenixville proper, of course, but it merits mentioning as part of its discussion.

As a final verdict, Phoenixville is immersed in some interesting history, lore, and legends—especially when you also consider the outlying area—but I believe it falls short of West Chester when it comes to the idea of being haunted or eerie. If you're keeping score for some reason, there you have it.

# SIX

More Ghosts and Legends
at the Inn

Just when you thought we'd run through all the spirited inns and taverns of Chester County, you're getting pulled back in for more. What gives here, anyway?

Blame American curiosity and the adventurous spirit propagated by the whole "manifest destiny" argument, as the push west from densely populated areas such as Philadelphia resulted in the creation of smaller rural pockets for a century or two. And where there are people, they'll need some place to wet their whistles to either drown their sorrows or celebrate their achievements, which is in line with Homer Simpson's theory of alcohol being "the cause of, and solution to, all of life's problems." That being said, it felt appropriate to break up the inns and public houses of Chester County into two separate chapters, if only to keep it from getting stale and redundant. Although, if you ask me, I could hang around atmospheric old taverns all the time and not get bored. The beer probably helps with that, though.

Inns, taverns, and the like afford you a cozy seat where you can take your time soaking in the environs and converse with others. Or sit in the corner, being a creepy shadow figure, if you prefer. Here you will find some unique tales of spirits unwilling to depart this world, as well as some interesting histories of the buildings themselves. So let's belly up to the bar for one final chapter of this trek through Chester County's rich—and sometimes lurid—past to see if we can uncover any more unsettling, eerie, or otherwise notable parts of it.

Last call.

# Dilworthtown Inn

Location: 1388 Old Wilmington Pike, West Chester
39.89993, −75.56750

We are barely squeezing this one in, since it sits just on the Chester County side of a county line that zigzags through the area. Additionally, the historic Dilworthtown Inn and its surrounding buildings are undergoing a dramatic transformation as of this writing.

After the first structure was built on this property in the 1750s, another was added some years later. Since then, "the Inn has seen more than 230 years of American history. Its monikers have included the Sign of the Pennsylvania Farmer, the Black Horse Tavern, Sign of the Rising Sun and Cross Keys, receiving its present name in 1821" (Pisasale 2021). It was during these early days that the Dilworthtown Inn found itself very close to ground zero during the fierce fighting of the Battle of Brandywine.

Owner Charles Dilworth saw the British take over his property and use it as a makeshift jail, eventually causing a large amount of damage. The nearby building, which later became the Blue Pear Bistro, was also said to be used as a temporary hospital, which no doubt would have seen suffering and loss of life. It is no wonder, then, that there have been reports of ghosts of the past at the Dilworthtown. "The root cellar has been turned into an extensive wine cellar, and waiters have heard voices down there. Employees have seen doors open and close, and found chairs facing each other as if someone was engaged in conversation. One server mistook a wounded soldier spirit for a customer after hours" (Bigham and Hudson 2013). An oak tree near the tavern was also the site of at least one reported execution by hanging, which only adds to the haunted vibes around the property.

In her book *Inns, Tales and Taverns of Chester County* (1984), Meg Twaddell recounts a haunting tale of yesteryear, an interaction at the Dilworthtown that occurred on September 26, 1778, between Squire Thomas Cheyney and Charles Dilworth concerning "the charmed but tragic life of James Fitzpatrick" (p. 107). "Sandy Flash" had just gone to the gallows, much to the delight of the vitriolic Dilworth but to the very mixed emotions of Cheyney, who did not view Fitzpatrick so harshly, nor was he predisposed to celebrate death to begin with. Cheyney had spoken to Fitzpatrick's beloved, a woman named Rachel, right around the time of his execution, and he had gained a deeper understanding of Fitz's overall personality rather than just focusing on his reputation as a lawbreaker and turncoat. It is difficult to ascertain how historically accurate this all was, but it is nevertheless a fine retelling and reflection that puts you in the mindset of the day and gives you a sense of the deep history of this inn.

The Dilworthtown Inn and its sister properties the Blue Pear Bistro and the Innkeeper's Kitchen went dark after the death of longtime steward Jim Barnes in 2019, but the whole complex is being reimagined for future generations to enjoy. A plant-based restaurant/bar/market has already opened, and arrangements are being made to bring other eateries into the fold, along with event spaces and possibly other retail.

One would hope that the Dilworthtown stays as close to its familiar form as possible. It has a lot of history to tell within its walls and on its grounds, both living and otherwise.

# Eagle Tavern

Location: 123 Pottstown Pike, Chester Springs
40.07825, −75.68848

Dating to the 1700s, this historical building has had a fair share of local history walk through its doors, including frequent visits by James Fitzpatrick. Yes, our pal Sandy Flash yet again. The history of the Eagle is a bit convoluted, so here is a quick rundown:

1702: Construction of the original building

1727: Liquor license issued, becomes a tavern

1799: Current building built over the original structure, renamed the "President Adams" (reverted back to "Eagle" later on)

1850s: May or may not have been torn down and replaced with a newer structure (but most accounts stick with the 1799 date)

Over the course of its run, the Eagle has also held the monikers "Little Eagle" and "Spread Eagle," but it has largely been known just by its simpler name. Some of its earliest legends concern Captain Fitz himself, when he was the head of an outlaw group known as the Doan Gang. On one occasion, some fifty men who were trying to track him down gave up on their quarry for the evening and went to the Eagle to regroup:

As they sat mulling over the fruitless outcome of their search, the tavern door swung open and Fitz, wheeling a long[-]nosed rifle, stood grinning defiantly at his audience. He pleasantly instructed all of them to keep their seats, declaring he would shoot the first one who moved. After drinking down a small glass of rum, he walked backward a few paces, bid them farewell, and took to his heels. The bounty hunters sat in silent amazement (Twaddell 1984, 93).

It is also said that the Eagle was the site of a shoot-out between American troops and the Doan Gang, where Fitz and his posse were nearly captured but escaped largely intact. This was, of course, before James Fitzpatrick would ultimately meet his gruesome end via the hangman's noose (and the hangman himself).

One of the more commonly spread and modern tales of the unexplained at the Eagle concerns a female patron who went to use the bathroom. Upon entering the women's room, she found its two stalls unoccupied and chose one of them. While using it, and despite not having heard anyone enter the bathroom behind her, she had a sudden feeling that someone was there. She leaned over to look under the partition that was separating the two stalls, and, at that point, she saw what she described as "black old-fashioned shoes." Instinct kicked in for her: she decided that she did not have to use the facilities so badly after all, and she left the bathroom in a hurry.

True to form for a dining establishment that has seen many staff members pass through over the years, some of them have laid blame on a resident ghost whenever items fall, are seemingly moved on their own, or otherwise disappear. The third floor, which consists of offices and storage, seems to have a particular presence about it, and employees say that they just keep doors closed and have learned to ignore any odd activity. It has also been said that passersby have seen a woman in a red dress in one of the third-story windows. Needless to say, this woman is not of this earthly plane. And then there is Mary Anne, who worked at the Eagle in the 1980s but lost her head (and life, of course) in a snowmobile accident one evening when a local was giving employees rides home during a blizzard. As a result, Mary Anne's spirit is still trapped at the Eagle to this day.

The basement has also been a prominent spot for some general disturbances and unexplained sounds. This could be related to the existence of tunnels underneath the building, which are believed to have been used as part of the Underground Railroad. These tunnels have been sealed off, but the history below your feet remains frozen in time.

A fire in 2010 nearly brought the old place down, but it was resurrected and reopened a few months later. As of this writing, the famed Eagle Tavern building is home to the Bloom Southern Kitchen restaurant, an establishment that opened its doors in 2020 and serves what you might call "elevated comfort food." It has been updated inside and out to reflect its new theming, but it retains its historical charm and overall look of its time period. Whether or not it still preserves an atmosphere of something otherworldly might be up to the individual beholder. My bartender did mention that there was an open tab for a "James Fitzpatrick," and I'm only half convinced that he was joking.

# Seven Stars Inn

Location: 263 Hoffecker Road, Phoenixville
40.16407, −75.59634

The long history of the Seven Stars Inn is rivaled in richness only by the food that they serve up on a nightly basis. And no, this isn't an advertisement for them.

The historical mastermind behind this place is a man by the name of Gerhard Brumbach, a local farmer who was a well-liked member of his community. The building was constructed sometime around 1720 as his home, then converted into a public house (or "publick house" in ye olde King's English) a few years later after he got tired of entertaining travelers in his residence without being able to at least make some money out of it. Business boomed.

After Gerhard's death years later, his son Benjamin inherited the business, then Benjamin's son Henry carried on the family legacy after him. Henry died in 1804, at which point the tavern changed hands and left the family. It was bought by a man named John Baker, who then dubbed it "Seven Stars," and the name has gone unchanged in the two centuries since.

It is even said that George Washington visited the inn shortly after the Battle of Brandywine. His troops were most definitely in the area, and it would have made sense for him to cool his heels or hold a meeting at such a place. But like many of the other locales we have come across, there is a dark history to the inn. Going back to its founding Brumbach family, Benjamin Brownback (his name had been "Americanized" from Brumbach) died in 1786. Nothing odd there. But just a short time later, his widow, Rachel Parker, was murdered in the stables behind the building. The questions as to "Who?" and "Why?" were never answered.

As you could have guessed, Rachel supposedly still hangs around the inn to this day. There are vague reports of a female presence watching over people and even going so far as to make an impression in furniture, as if the entity were sitting down to have a chat with someone. You'd have to think that this is Rachel, still milling about the building where she spent so much time with her husband while they were alive. Apparently, nothing malicious goes on, but it's still enough to make you think twice about being in the building alone at any point.

A former custodian seems to have experienced the worst of it, which makes sense, given how much time she spent on the property. She reported looking up a staircase and seeing a young person dressed in a riding outfit, someone who should not have been there at the time. Just as quickly the apparition vanished before her eyes. The spirit's clothing may have been tied to the fact that Rachel Parker had been killed in the stables, but there is no way to take it any further than that.

On another occasion the same former custodian was nudged by an unseen force while at work. Possibly related to this, a medium detected the presence of a man lying on the floor. This may lend some credibility to a tale that had been circulated about a former owner of the inn who either dropped dead inside the building or died from a fall down the stairs (which, I suppose, is also technically "dropping dead"). The connection is tenuous. On top of all this, a young boy has also been spotted at the Seven Stars, although no stories have ever emerged about how he might fit into the building's past. There aren't any great explanations to these various sightings, but they have piled up over the years.

The third floor offers still more potential activity, since a former waitress at the Seven Stars reported that she once followed someone who appeared to be one of her fellow employees up the stairs, only ever seeing them from the back. Upon arriving at the top of the stairs, this supposed person then went into an adjoining room, never to reemerge. The attic above this floor also purportedly hosted the hanging suicide of a young woman many years ago, leaving one to wonder if the entity that disappeared on the third floor was the same unfortunate individual, now trapped on the upper levels of the inn for all time.

Many people have reported feelings of unease and a general eeriness throughout this structure, rendering it as seemingly one of the oldest and creepiest places in the county, which is saying something. Keep that in mind the next time you find yourself at the Seven Stars. As you hack into your king's cut filet mignon, you may be dining in the presence of more than just your party at the table.

# Blue Ball Inn

## Location: Russell and Old Lancaster Roads, Berwyn
## 40.04369, −75.46119

More than probably any other historic tavern in Chester County, the Blue Ball Inn (not to be confused with Montgomery County's Blue *Bell* Inn) has a well-documented sordid and strange history. And this is due solely to one person—its former proprietress, Prissy Robinson.

Prissy, proper name Priscilla Moore Robinson, ruled the roost at the Blue Ball for decades after it came into her possession when she inherited it from her mother. Having been built sometime around 1735, the Blue Ball Inn was already a well-known waypoint for travelers at that time, having ushered a couple of generations of them through its doors as its ownership changed hands every few years. Once Prissy was in charge, though, she definitely put her own stamp on the place, as she quickly established a no-nonsense and stern reputation.

Over the years this reputation was no doubt aided by the fact that Prissy had an—pardon the expression—"old hag" look going on, which was scary to the kids in the region and helped propagate the narrative about her. But maybe the local youth were on to something here. Furthering the mystique surrounding her and the Blue Ball, all three of Prissy's husbands were said to have disappeared, as did some of the guests at the inn. This in turn led to even more stories being spread about what the proprietress of the Blue Ball was up to. According to Hager (2006),

> Legend has it that guests would sometimes be awakened by muffled cries in the night and scraping noises, like that of a shovel on hard dirt, only to be served steaming black coffee and sugared doughnuts by Prissy in the morning. One wealthy woman was found hung [sic] at the inn and Prissy claimed it to be suicide. (p. 110)

Might this woman have flashed too much cash and caught Prissy's eye as a target? It has been strongly implied that Prissy did just this sort of thing on a number of occasions. No matter what, though, Prissy clearly had no misgivings about putting random people in danger. She is said to have been so furious that one of her farm animals was killed when it was struck by a passing train on the new railroad tracks right by her property in the 1830s that she began greasing the tracks (possibly with grease that she made from the animal itself) until the railroad reimbursed her for the lost animal. Thankfully, the greasing led only to delays and inconvenience for travelers, not an all-out derailment.

After Prissy died and her reign (of terror?) came to an end, the inn struggled to keep up operations. It changed ownership a few times and was essentially driven out of business by the railroad, as patronage from passing travelers waned. The Blue Ball was turned into a private residence in 1894, but the ghosts of the past remained within its walls and on the property. Ms. Mary Croasdale, who owned and lived in the home for over fifty years, reported regular knocking on doors and windows, as well as drawers of chests opening and closing on their own for no reason, unless of course it was because Prissy needed new clothes after staining her garments with blood.

In addition, Ms. Croasdale said that she saw curtains moving in a room with no open windows or other source of air, and she also experienced an occasional light touch on her arms and shoulders, the kind of thing that seems to have become so commonplace with this type of reported activity. Heavy knocking on doors, a clock in perfect condition that stopped for no reason, and doors swinging open on their own are just some of the other strange happenings that have been experienced over the decades and were pinned on Prissy.

Another story goes on to say that some years after Prissy's passing, a house down the road from the Blue Ball that had once been part of the tavern property burned down. A local man went to photograph the ruins:

The man focused his camera and took a shot of the old wall with the ruined stairs leading upward into nothing. When the photo was developed, he was shocked. The photograph clearly showed an old woman standing on the ruined stairs. The woman was bent over with age, and she wore a long dress and a large bonnet. Was it Prissy revisiting a familiar place? (Nesbitt 2008, 65)

Prissy's legend would grow even more when, during renovations to put in a garden behind the house, six human skeletons were reportedly found buried underneath the kitchen or the cellar, since sources conflict. Were these unsuspecting travelers, or even inn workers, that Prissy had robbed and murdered? Had some of them been killed in an alcohol-induced fight and simply been disposed of rather than involving the authorities? We'll never know for certain, but Prissy undoubtedly "knew where the bodies were buried" at the very least, if not being the direct cause of them. One sensationalistic source even offered up this scenario of how Prissy may have done away with peddlers who were carrying large amounts of money:

Before the great fireplace in the old kitchen Prissy would serve them steaming suppers along with a glass of hot rum. When these same peddlers went up to the room over the kitchen, they would find a keg of whiskey and a pannikin beside the bed. After partaking freely of the whiskey they would be in a sleep too deep to be roused by the stealthy figure that would creep in the door. A quick sharp blow—and another limp figure would be dragged down the narrow stairs, to be hidden until a shallow grave could be dug in the beaten earth floor of the kitchen or in the orchard. (Patterson 1952)

Prissy is said to have run her establishment all the way up until her death in 1877, at the ripe old age of one hundred, her surly nature somehow managing to carry her past the century mark. She is buried about 4 miles away from her former property, at the Great Valley Presbyterian Church Cemetery in Malvern. Her plain stone is marked only with her married name (one of them, at least), "Priscilla Robinson Cahill," and her dates of birth and death.

More-recent owners of the property have reported hearing knocking on doors and feet shuffling over the floors, as well as one instance when a "housekeeper resigned one day after feeling an 'ironlike grip' on her shoulder" (Twaddell 1984, 21), with the family dog thereafter beginning to act strangely in the room where this had occurred.

Today, the building that once hosted so many travelers as the Blue Ball Inn is catty-corner from a SEPTA station, which is fitting, but also an odd juxtaposition. Most people coming in and out of this busy commuting area have no idea about the importance and the history of the structure just a few hundred feet away. It's hoped that Prissy has reconciled herself to this fact, because it seems that we should try not to make her too upset. Best of luck to the current residents of this building.

# Turk's Head Tavern

## Location: 3 North High Street, West Chester
## 39.95994, −75.60413

In its earliest incarnation, the town of West Chester was known as Turk's Head (or sometimes Turks Head without the apostrophe), and its hub was no doubt the eponymous tavern in the center of town.

The Turk's Head faced East Market Street, although the building that occupies the site today has a much-larger footprint and a North High Street address. The name, in case you were wondering, is traced back to the Crusades. It seems that English Crusaders were in the practice of bringing the heads of their defeated foes back with them and displaying them for the public. With social media unavailable at the time, signs were created to advertise this morbid curiosity, and the practice stuck, leading to many taverns and public houses in Britain taking up this name over the centuries that followed. The custom carried over into the New World. Cute, right?

For a time, West Chester's version of the Turk's Head was essentially the only option for travelers making their way to or from Philadelphia, Wilmington, or any larger city within wagon-driving distance, so it did quite well in the food, drink, and hospitality business. People, companies, and technology came and went in West Chester, but for almost two hundred years, the Turk's Head existed in some form or another as part of the community that had thrived around it until it was finally razed in the latter half of the twentieth century.

If you swing over to the East Market Street side of the bank building that currently sits at the address, you will be greeted by two large, Ten Commandments–like tablets that were affixed to the side of the building in 1965. One of the markers discusses the Dime Savings Bank of Chester County, and the other dips its toes into the history of the tavern that stood there. It reads:

TURK'S HEAD TAVERN

1769-1964

This bank occupies the site on which John Hoopes erected the Turk's Head Tavern in 1769.

Much of West Chester's early history is associated with the Turk's Head.

For nearly 200 years, as tavern and hotel, it was an important center for military, political, and social discussions.

Stock of Chester County banks was often sold at public auction from the hotel porch.

The tavern lasted for many years, but most of its spirit activity dates back to its very early days, when it was one of the few local meeting places that existed during the American Revolution. As the story goes, a number of wounded American troops were brought to the Turk's Head a few days after the Battle of Brandywine in 1777, since the tavern had been turned into a hospital to tend to the wounded. The next day, more Redcoats arrived, hot in pursuit of some fleeing Continental soldiers. A skirmish broke out on September 16 that carried into the next day. According to Sarro's *Ghosts of West Chester* (2008),

> The troops that had died as a result of the skirmish were buried in a schoolyard that was across from the Turks Head Tavern and it is believed to be where the municipal building now stands at the corner of Market and High Streets in the heart of West Chester. On the anniversary of this event, if you stand on the corner of High and Market Streets, you may just hear the gunshots and cries of the soldiers past. (p. 23)

There also exists a story that a disembodied "guardian angel" saved the embattled colonials from further disaster while they were in and around the Turk's Head. With one soldier doing a poor job of keeping watch and basically falling asleep on the job, he was startled awake by the voice of a young child warning him about approaching soldiers. It turned out that these were Hessian troops in service of the British, and the warning of this unknown voice prompted the Americans to act quickly enough to repel them. No explanation was ever given about where the warning came from.

Today, the legacy of the name lives on in local establishments such as Turk's Head Coffee Roasters and the Turks Head Café, and there's even an annual Turks Head Music Festival at Everhart Park. The tavern is just a memory, but its impact will seemingly remain for as long as the borough of West Chester exists.

# Octoraro Hotel

## Location: 2 South 3rd Street, Oxford
## 39.78506, −75.97910

This historic brick building situated near the end of Oxford's pleasant main drag goes by many nicknames, so one can be forgiven if they are not totally clear on the subject being discussed.

Not to be confused with the old Oxford Hotel just across the street, which has been divided into apartments, the Octoraro Hotel building is the site of the current Octoraro Tavern, which is the latest in a line of watering holes to be housed within this edifice. Locals might call it by either the name of the building or the name of the tavern, or simply "the Octoraro." Or they might go all the way to calling it the "OTE" (as in "oat"), thanks to the vertical sign on the side of the building that clearly displays the words "THE OCTORARO OTE SINCE 1827." People might also call it "O.T.E." in reference to these letters.

At any rate, the sign was installed in 2018 in homage to a previous sign on the building's facade, one from which the letters "H" and "L" in the word "Hotel" disappeared sometime in the 1960s. Details are sketchy as to the reason for this, although you would think that folks would be able to pinpoint a weather event, garden variety vandalism, or something else. No matter how it ended up that way, the sign remained in this state for a long time, and the "OTE" moniker stuck. That's a fun little story, but it's not much for our purposes. Luckily, there is an otherworldly feel to this place as well. Because when it comes to the paranormal, let's just say that some elements inside this old building have enjoyed much more staying power than its exterior features.

While it was still operational as a hotel in the late 1990s, there was a fire in the building, which thankfully did not result in any loss of life but forced the brother of the owner to stay in a third-floor room after that point. He would go on to report the very distinctive sounds of footsteps, as you would expect if someone were pacing the hall and entering a room. Of course, nothing ever materialized from this auditory mystery. Doors were also heard to open and close, intermixed with the heavy steps, never to be explained.

Over the years the staff has had numerous encounters with and has even taken a shine to a ghost named "Eddie." There have been sightings of odd shadows in the hallway, lights around the bar flickering from time to time, and doors either opening ever so slightly or being slammed shut entirely. Eddie's disruptive and mischievous nature seems to be par for the course at the place, and workers just shrug and go about their business.

There has also been a sighting of a rather Victorian spirit at the Octoraro. A former cook was dealing with some strange occurrences in the kitchen, which he attributed to a tall gentleman whom he spotted on one occasion.

This man was fully dressed in nineteenth-century attire, with a high collar and top hat finishing the ensemble. This dapper fellow may be the one responsible for some activity experienced by staff in the hallway leading to the kitchen, as well as in the basement level of the property.

If you find yourself in Oxford, make time to stroll around the town and enjoy the throwback feel of its main thoroughfare. While you're there, you can also pull up a stool and "throw back" one at the bar of the Octoraro, or "the OTE" if you prefer. Shoot some pool; enjoy. Even if it's not all that busy, you still might find that you have company.

# Odds and Ends

Doing this kind of research, you discover all sorts of interesting tidbits and locales that are worth looking into, but ultimately don't have enough "going on" to merit an entire section. So allow me to point a few of these places out.

Archie's Corner, located on Ring Road in Chadds Ford, was a frequent visiting place for Andrew Wyeth, who would take in the scenery and work his magic with his artist's brush. Today, to passersby without any further knowledge, the area of Archie's Corner just looks like the ruins of a building. And, well, it is. But the octagonal schoolhouse that once sat on this site was an important structure in the community's history. There is a roadside plaque that furnishes you with more information, as well as a small cemetery to explore.

Another graveyard, the Derry African Union Cemetery, is found along South Caln Road in East Fallowfield Township. It is just one of the dozens of African American cemeteries found around Chester County that were largely lost to history, but some are being documented and restored as part of a worthy project. Some of these are now on private land, so keep that in mind if you ever plan to visit any of these cemeteries.

Moore Hall, on Valley Forge Road in Phoenixville, is just a cool old building with historical significance to our country. It hosted a Continental delegation for a period of time, including George Washington and our old pal Anthony Wayne, years before his escapade in the kettle. I had planned to dedicate more space to Moore Hall, but apparently no ghosts of the Revolution have decided to take up residence there, so it gets only a passing mention here.

The historic Vickers Tavern in Exton was formerly the home and workshop of local potter John Vickers during the mid-1800s, and it was also a stop on the Underground Railroad. The building operated as a restaurant for decades before closing in 2021, but as of this writing it will be reopening soon as a White Dog Café.

Chester County was also home to an early aviator, George Alexander Spratt. If you are ever on Reeceville Road in Coatesville, look for the historical marker that discusses how his early experiments influenced the Wright Brothers. In fact, look for historical markers anywhere you can find them across Chester County, which has well over four hundred of them. Places we've covered such as Phoenixville and West Chester account for many, but there are plenty to be found in Kennett Square, Malvern, Chadds Ford, and beyond. I could keep going, but I will leave some of the investigating to you.

# Epilogue

*Webster's Dictionary* defines an epilogue as "a concluding section that rounds out the design of a literary work." So I guess I have to do one.

While I do realize that this is not the first book to tackle the spooky and strange history and sites of Chester County, nor will it be the last, thank you for joining me in my best attempt to make these stories and places more accessible to the people who reside here, and anyone from neighboring areas who might take an interest.

Chester County, Pennsylvania, really is a great place to live, visit, and explore. Yes, there are the busier and more-metropolitan areas of it, but some parts of it put me in the mind of an idyllic New England town, the closest you can get without actually being up that way. On the plus side, the winter weather here is not as extreme as in New England, and the regional accents here are slightly less terrible.

Living in an area so intertwined with American history and the birth of this nation goes a long way toward the civic pride that exists, and Chester County is home to many great artists, business minds, educators, and other important figures, in addition to amateurish authors. It is also far enough away from New Jersey that people can breathe a little easier when they are here, whether they're studying at West Chester University, checking out the many fine restaurants, or getting engaged at Longwood Gardens, which seems like such a great idea that I can't believe I'm definitely the first person to ever think of it.

Even if you don't actively seek out the stops that I've detailed in the "road trip" itinerary in the next section, I'd reckon that you would find something of note even if you drove somewhat aimlessly for a half hour or so anywhere around Chester County. All it takes is a curious mind, which you can fill with more information after consulting the computer in your hand or by using actual physical media, and you'll find that there are all sorts of stories hidden in the buildings, graveyards, and other sites around the general area.

I would always recommend reading roadside markers if you come upon them (and it's safe to stop and do so!) because you never know what it might spark within you. Chatting up some locals always helps too if you are the sort of person who is comfortable with that. You could pick up a new hobby, interest, or passion after you start to scratch the surface, which is really one of those "spice of life" things that we do not realize we are thankful for until it hits us over the head.

Chester County has orchards and preserves and a helicopter museum, and it is even home to a television shopping channel that used to be good. It is a great place to seek out American history, arts and literature, picturesque areas for photography, railroads, or maybe just some good ghost stories if that is what you're after. There's something for every interest if you make just a little bit of an effort, and if this book piqued or enhanced any such curiosity in its reader, then that is fantastic.

# Chester County "Ghosts & Legends" Road Trip

By grouping these haunted, odd, or otherwise notable sites by category rather than location throughout this book, I have left you with quite a scattershot mess. So how do we put this all together? Why, with an itinerary, of course. You will need to go to whatever website/app you choose to use for turn-by-turn directions, but here is a trip for you to undertake if you care to visit all the locations herein.

You can start your tour at any of the stops, on the basis of where you're coming from, because it is essentially a loop. Then just go back to the top of this travel plan. Think of it as being akin to a shotgun-start golf tournament. Begin at any point along the course, then just keep going until you've played all the holes and end up back where you started.

Some are admittedly more interesting or accessible than others. And some are more of the "quick stop" variety, while others are truly an experience that will take you some time. (Also, there is no precise location given for the Pennypacker tragedy, so I have omitted it from this list.) The important thing is to know that these places are out there, and that you do not have to go too far to find something that will interest you. Maybe the fact that these sorts of locales are here in your own backyard will inspire you to look for places farther afield. See as much as you can, I say. You'll never reach the end, but you'll stay engaged and find yourself looking forward to new adventures that don't need to have great costs or risks associated with them.

# Chester County Road Trip Stops

1. The Ticking Tomb (39.74649, −75.77500)
2. Letty's Tavern (39.84733, −75.71046)
3. Devil's Road (39.84738, −75.63403)
4. Brandywine Battlefield (39.87455, −75.57627)
5. Dilworthtown Inn (39.89993, −75.56750)
6. The Ghost in the Clock Tower (39.95973, −75.60509)
7. Turk's Head Tavern (39.95994, −75.60413)
8. Valley Creek Road Twin Tunnels (40.00467, −75.66556)
9. Exton Witch House (40.05786, −75.65021)
10. Ship Inn (40.03022, −75.61011)
11. Battle of the Clouds (40.04213, −75.57762)
12. General Warren Inn (40.04274, −75.52453)
13. Duffy's Cut (40.03704, −75.53201)
14. The Paoli Massacre (40.02958, −75.51917)
15. Blue Ball Inn (40.04369, −75.46119)
16. Mad Anthony Wayne (40.02728, −75.40468)
17. Valley Forge (40.10150, −75.42296)
18. Phoenixville Library (40.12885, −75.51412)
19. Seven Stars Inn (40.16407, −75.59634)
20. Pennhurst Asylum (40.19326, −75.56102)
21. Fricks Locks Village (40.22323, −75.59700)
22. Free Love Valley (40.22365, −75.70407)
23. Inn at St. Peter's Village (40.17801, −75.73099)
24. Eagle Tavern (40.07825, −75.68848)
25. The Dorlan Devil (40.04763, −75.71726)
26. Potter's Field (39.93761, −75.72992)
27. Doe Run Village (39.91592, −75.81772)
28. Stottsville Inn (39.95977, −75.88819)
29. Red Rose Inn (39.82420, −75.87003)
30. Octoraro Hotel (39.78506, −75.97910)

# Acknowledgments

I'll start by thanking two very different writers for helping shape my style and voice over the past few years. First, to J. W. (Jason) Ocker, whose book *Poe-Land* I picked up sometime around 2015 and whose work I have not stopped reading since. It's been great to follow your exploits, communicate with you online, and meet you on a few occasions. Thank you for showing me a side of writing and general passion for those odd and offbeat parts of life that I believed was in me somewhere but didn't know how to focus. I also really liked the format of your book *Cursed Objects* and used it as a model for this book, since it seemed very appropriate for this kind of subject matter. From travelogues to middle-grade horror, J. W. is talented across the board, and he's a friend.

And to Sean McIndoe, a hockey writer for *The Athletic* whom I have also been reading for almost a decade. You'll probably never read this, and I'll probably never meet you, but your style of wit and "humour" (as they call it in Canada) have kept me coming back for more. Your way of perfectly blending two of my favorite things—the sport of hockey and being as sarcastic as possible—has been a master class.

As for people who know me on a more personal level, my great friends Bill Paulino and Mike Brown leap to mind, since they have dealt with my musings, writings, and ramblings for many years. Your friendship and continued encouragement fuel me. I look forward to several more decades of joking around with you. As for Matt Juliano, Christine Snow-Opio, Lindsay Mundth, and the "Wednesday Knight" street hockey guys from the Jennersville YMCA, you all rock as well. Thank you so much for being there for me over the years. I could name many other folks, but I don't want this to ramble on for too long.

Thank you so much to the great team at Schiffer Publishing, especially Carey Massimini, Dinah Roseberry, and Ian Robertson, for making this book a reality and giving me my first opportunity to become a published author. It has been an awesome experience and I am happy to be part of the team.

Mom and Dad, as I get older, I become even more appreciative of the life you gave me. I'm sure it wasn't easy, but please know that you aced the parenting test. Any successes that I have wouldn't have been possible without you. I love you.

To my wife, Rachael, who took the cover photo for my first book but to whom I didn't give any credit; sorry about that. But you're the best wife and mother around, and I hope I tell you that enough to make up for all the stuff that I put you through. Thank you also for your unwavering support, and for the proofreading and editing help. Love always to my best friend.

My boys, Nolan and Griffin, you make everything worth it. I'd work a hundred hours a week in a coal mine if it meant that I could still be your dad and watch you grow up into fine young men. Of course, I'd prefer not to work myself into an early grave if I can help it, so don't call my bluff. Either way, my love for you is unconditional.

See you all around Chester County.

# Bibliography

Adams, Charles. *Ghost Stories of Chester County and the Brandywine Valley*. Wyomissing, PA: Exeter House Books, 2001.

Adams, Charles. *Great Train Wrecks of Eastern Pennsylvania*. Wyomissing, PA: Exeter House Books, 1992.

"America's Scariest Tunnels? The Twin Tunnels of Downingtown, Pennsylvania May Take the Prize." The Lineup Staff. Last modified December 15, 2017. https://the-line-up.com/the-twin-tunnels-of-downingtown-pennsylvania.

"Anthony 'Mad Anthony' Wayne." FindAGrave.com. Accessed December 2023. www.findagrave.com/memorial/2711/anthony-wayne.

Bell, J. L. "The Legends of Sandy Flash Drive." Last modified January 15, 2020. https://boston1775.blogspot.com/2020/01/the-legends-of-sandy-flash-drive.html.

Benshoff, Laura. "Honoring Black Civil War Vets Buried in Neglect, Chester Community Moves to Restore Cemetery." Last modified March 3, 2016. https://whyy.org/articles/to-honor-black-civil-war-vets-buried-in-neglect-chester-community-rallies-to-restore-cemetery/.

Bigham, Mary, and Leslie Hudson. "Haunted Restaurants of Chester County." Last modified October 2013. www.PAeats.org.

Chadderdon, Jesse. "Historic Oxford Hotel the Unlikely Epicenter of Chester County's Music Scene." *News Journal*, May 26, 2009. https://www.delawareonline.com/story/entertainment/arts/2009/05/26/historic-oxford-hotel-unlikely-epicenter/63946505007/.

Chambless, J. "The Potter's Field, a Forgotten Piece of Local History." *Chester County Press*, May 16, 2018. https://www.chestercounty.com/2018/05/16/173361/the-potters-field-a-forgotten-piece-of-local-history.

"Chester County Alms House Cemeteries." FindAGrave.com. Accessed December

2023. www.findagrave.com/ceme-tery/2183716/chester-county-alms-house-cemeteries.

"Chester County's Poorhouse." *The Hunt.* Accessed December 2023. www.thehuntmagazine.com/feature/chester-countys-poorhouse.

Coia, Gabe. "Mulliner the Mariner: The Man beyond the Myth." Last modified January 23, 2015. https://www.njpinebarrens.com/mulliner-the-mariner-the-man-be-yond-the-myth/.

Craig, Keith. "West Chester Legends." Last modified December 2023. https://www.bluetoad.com/publication/?i=4468&article_id=39758&view=articleBrowser.

D'Angelo, Joe. "There's Paranormal Activity at Historic Stottsville Inn." *Daily Local News,* November 20, 2008. https://www.dailylocal.com/2008/11/20/theres-paranormal-activity-at-histor-ic-stottsville-inn-2/.

"Derry Union American Methodist Episcopal Cemetery." FindAGrave.com. Accessed December 2023. www.findagrave.com/cemetery/2224473/hutchinson-memorial-union-ameri-can-methodist-episcopal-cemetery.

DeVan, Kathryn. "Our Most Famous Border: The Mason-Dixon Line." Pennsylvania Center for the Book. Last modified December 2023. https://pabook.libraries.psu.edu/literary-cultural-heritage-map-pa/feature-articles/our-most-famous-border-mason-dix-on-line.

Dixon, Mark. *The Hidden History of Chester County: Lost Tales from the Delaware & Brandywine Valleys.* Charleston, SC: History Press, 2011.

Dixon, Mark. "Reexamining the Story behind Indian Hannah." Last modified December 13, 2017. https://mainlinetoday.com/life-style/reexamining-the-story-behind-indi-an-hannah/.

"1877–Oct 4, Tropical Storm Flooding, Rails Wash Out, Train Derails, near Kimberton, PA-11." US Deadly Events. Accessed December 2023. https://www.usdeadlyevents.com/1877-oct-4-tropical-storm-flood-ing-rails-wash-out-train-derails-near-kimberton-pa-11/.

F, Rick. "Indian Hannah and the Stargazers Stone." RSF Trip Reporter. Last modified September 27, 2013. https://rsftripreporter.net/indian-hannah-stargazers-stone/.

Gaw, Richard. "Oxford Hotel Damaged in Tuesday Blaze." *Chester County Press,* November 6, 2014. https://www.chestercounty.com/2014/11/06/50114/octoraro-hotel-damaged-in-tues-day-blaze.

"Good News Productions." Historical Marker Database. Accessed December 2023. https://www.hmdb.org/m.asp?m=35964.

Green, Jennifer. *Dark History of Penn's Woods: Murder, Madness & Misadventure in Southeastern Pennsylvania.* Havertown, PA: Brookline Books, 2021.

Hager, Caroline. "The Blue Ball Inn of Tredyffrin Township." *Tredyffrin Easttown History Quarterly* 43, no. 4 (Fall 2006): 107–11. https://www.tehistory.org/hqda/html/v43/v43n4p107.html.

"Hannah Shingle's Ghost." This Haunted Place. Accessed December 2023. http://thishauntedplace.com/content/hannah-shingles-ghost.

"Haunted Lancaster: The Ghost of General 'Mad Anthony' Wayne and His Missing Bones." Uncharted Lancaster. Last modified October 10, 2021. https://unchartedlancaster.com/2021/10/10/haunted-lancaster-mad-antho-nys-missing-ghostly-bones/.

"Hauntings of West Chester." Chester County Community Foundation. Accessed November 2023. www.chescocf.org/hauntings-of-west-chester/.

Hoffman, Elizabeth. *In Search of Ghosts: Haunted Places in the Delaware Valley.* Philadelphia: Camino Books, 1992.

Hoffman, Steven. "Investigating Ghosts in Kennett Square." *Chester County Press,* June 21, 2016. https://www.chester-county.com/2016/06/21/114696/investigating-ghosts-in-kennett-square.

Hoffman, Steven. "The Mystery of the Ticking Tomb—Examining Famous Local Legend near Landenberg." *Chester County Press,* October 19, 2020. https://www.chestercounty.com/2020/10/19/332059/the-mystery-of-the-ticking-tomb-examining-famous-local-legend-near-landenberg.

Hoffman, Steven. "A Stroll through Oxford's History." *Chester County Press,* August 27, 2014. https://www.chestercounty.com/2014/08/27/45866/a-stroll-through-oxford-s-history.

Hoppe, Jonathan. "Of Prisoners and Potter's Fields." Last modified August 23, 2021. https://www.chestercounty-day.com/articles/of-prisoners-and-potters-fields.

Hull, Laurie. *Brandywine Valley Ghosts: Haunts of Southeastern Pennsylvania.* Atglen, PA: Schiffer, 2008.

Johnson, Carl. "Phoenixville Phriday: The Pennypacker Tragedy." Last modified August 26, 2016. https://hoxsie.org/2016/08/26/phoenixville-phriday-the-pennypacker-tragedy/.

Kashatus, William. *Just over the Line: Chester County and the Underground Railroad.* West Chester, PA: Chester County Historical Society, 2002.

Katovitch, Diana. "Who Should Tell the Story? The Pennhurst Haunted Asylum and the Pennhurst Museum in Public History." Last modified June 7, 2022. https://ncph.org/history-at-work/who-should-tell-the-story-pennhurst-haunted-asylum/.

"Keeping History Alive with 3 Simple Letters." Historic Downtown Oxford Pennsylvania. Last modified February 12, 2019. www.downtownoxfordpa.org.

Kelly, Antoinette. "Newly Unearthed Remains at Duffy's Cut Offer New Information on Irish Laborers." Last modified October 16, 2011. https://www.irishcentral.com/roots/newly-unearthed-remains-at-duffys-cut-offer-new-information-on-irish-laborers-131945108-237418131.

Kovach, Emily. "Love a Good Scare? Check Out These 7 Reportedly Haunted Restaurants in PA." Last modified October 31, 2023. https://www.paeats.org/news/2023/haunted-restaurants-in-pa/.

Lanyon, Mark DeWitt. *Lost Chester County, Pennsylvania.* Charleston, SC: History Press, 2023.

Lindak, Virginia. "Uncovering Murder on the Main Line and the Victims of Duffy's Cut." Last modified October 28, 2020. https://hiddencityphila.org/2020/10/uncovering-murder-on-the-main-line-and-the-victims-of-duffys-cut/.

Littrell, Austin, and Mackenzie Taylor. "Chester County's Scary Stories and Haunted Tours." Last modified September 28, 2023. https://countylinesmagazine.com/article/chester-countys-scary-stories-and-haunted-tours/.

*Main Line Today* Staff. "Standing on Sandy's Shoulders." Last modified July 10, 2008. https://mainlinetoday.com/life-style/frontline-retrospect-8/.

McIndoe, Mary. Chester County Genealogy. https://chestercountygenealogy.com/modules/content/index.php?id=8, 2006.

Mikulich, Leah. "New 155-Unit Housing Project Could Be Coming to East Coventry." Last modified September 30, 2023. https://vista.today/2023/09/villages-at-fricks-lock-housing/.

Miyashiro, Nicole. "Claude Rains." Pennsylvania Center for the Book. Accessed November 2023. https://pabook.libraries.psu.edu/

literary-cultural-heritage-map-pa/
bios/Rains_Claude.

Mowday, Bruce. *Jailing the Johnston Gang: Bringing Serial Murderers to Justice*. Fort Lee, NJ: Barricade Books, 2009.

Mowday, Bruce. *West Chester: Six Walking Tours*. Atglen, PA: Schiffer, 2006.

Nesbitt, Mark, and Patty Wilson. *The Big Book of Pennsylvania Ghost Stories*. Mechanicsburg, PA: Stackpole Books, 2008.

Ocker, J. W. *The United States of Cryptids: A Tour of American Myths and Monsters*. Philadelphia: Quirk Books, 2022.

Park, Katie. "A Chester County Village Was Vacated for a Nuclear Power Plant. Today, It's a Ghost Town." *Philadelphia Inquirer*, August 3, 2018. https://www.inquirer.com/philly/news/pennsylvania/fricks-locks-village-ghost-town-exelon-limerick-east-coventry-20180803.html.

Patterson, Emma C. "Blue Ball Inn Layout, Owners: Bernhard Vauleer, Prissy Robinson, Croasdale, Wagner Families, Skeletons Unearthed, Ghosts." May 2, 1952. https://radnorhistory.org/archive/articles/ytmt/?p=190.

Patton, William, III. "Duffy's Cut: The Murder Mystery of Malvern." Pennsylvania Center for the Book. Accessed December 2023. https://pabook.libraries.psu.edu/literary-cultural-heritage-map-pa/feature-articles/duffys-cut-murder-mystery-malvern.

Penn Township. "Red Rose Inn." Accessed December 2023. www.penntownship.us/about/pages/red-rose-inn.

"Pennhurst Asylum." US Ghost Adventures. Accessed November 2023. https://usghostadventures.com/haunted-places/americas-most-haunted-hospitals-and-asylums/pennhurst-asylum/.

"Pennhurst State's Haunted History." Travel Channel. Accessed November 2023. https://www.travelchannel.com/shows/ghost-adventures/articles/pennhurst-states-haunted-history.

Pirmann, J. Gregory, and the Pennhurst Memorial & Preservation Alliance. *Pennhurst State School and Hospital*. Charleston, SC: Arcadia, 2015.

Pirro, J. F. "This Local Coroner Has Questions about the Duffy's Cut Mass Grave Site." Last modified August 8, 2019. https://mainlinetoday.com/life-style/this-local-coroner-still-has-questions-about-the-duffys-cut-mass-grave-site/.

Pisasale, Gene. "Living History: A Restaurant's Name, a Country's History." *Daily Local News*, August 19, 2021. https://www.dailylocal.com/2013/02/15/living-history-a-restaurants-name-a-countrys-history/.

"Prissy Robinson's Blue Ball Inn." This Haunted Place. Accessed December 2023. http://thishauntedplace.com/content/prissy-robinsons-blue-ball-inn.

Rellehan, Michael. "Daily Local News: Star Gazers' Stone More Accessible to Visitors." Last modified July 29, 2013. https://natlands.org/news/daily-local-news-star-gazers-stone-more-accessible-to-visitors/.

Roseberry, D. P. *Ghosts of Valley Forge and Phoenixville*. Atglen, PA: Schiffer, 2007.

Sarro, Mark. *Ghosts of West Chester, Pennsylvania*. Atglen, PA: Schiffer, 2008.

"SATANVILLE (Pennsbury Twp., Chester County)." TreasureNet. Last modified January 22, 2009. https://www.treasurenet.com/threads/satanville-pennsbury-twp-chester-county.112785/.

Scheib, Clyde. *West Seven Stars and Beyond: Preserving Local History*. Self-published: A&EM, 2020.

Schlosser, S. E. *Spooky Pennsylvania: Tales of Hauntings, Strange Happenings, and Other Local Lore*. Essex, CT: Globe Pequot, 2007.

Schuylkill Township. "Moore Hall." Accessed December 2023. https://schuylkilltwp.org/197/Moore-Hall.

Simonich, Milan. "Escape Revives a Town's Bad Memories." *Pittsburgh Post-Gazette*, August 15, 1999.

Smith, Sandy. "Just Listed: Historic Sharples House in West Chester." September 26, 2019. https://www.phillymag.com/property/2019/09/26/house-for-sale-west-chester-sharples-house/.

"The Star Gazers' Stone." Historical Marker Database. Accessed December 2023. https://www.hmdb.org/m.asp?m=159604.

Sweeney, Sara, host. "Brandywine Battlefield in Chadds Ford, PA: Spectral Steeds and Silent Guardians." *Paranormal in Pennsylvania*. Podcast audio, season 1, episode 3, February 1, 2023. https://open.spotify.com/episode/2S8jjtTuPp5UaOKY-44WqSo?si=SPT61i4TScmQ_XR0Xv_YGQ.

Sweeney, Sara, host. "Pennhurst State School and Hospital in Chester County, PA: Hands off the Airplane!" *Paranormal in Pennsylvania*. Podcast audio, season 1, episode 6, February 1, 2023, https://open.spotify.com/episode/6W8HLTzZJbRROLasB-n3ie6?si=MLYkTlD9RlS971kK-flmdfQ.

Sweeney, Sara, and Erica Barrett, hosts. "Exton Witch House in Exton, PA: Enchanted Estate or Family Farmhouse?" *Paranormal in Pennsylvania*. Podcast audio, season 3, episode 12, January 4, 2024, https://open.spotify.com/episode/3DRDILJBa4YY1JOB-HeB6mn?si=-AP26lZ_T26EIvFKgps8uw.

Talorico, Patricia. "New Haunt? Historic Kennett Tavern Offers Food, Drinks and a Ghost." *Delaware News Journal*, April 22, 2021. https://www.delawareonline.com/story/life/food/2021/04/22/lettys-tavern-food-drinks-ghost-william-penns-daughter/7282376002/.

Tassin, Susan. *Pennsylvania Ghost Towns: Uncovering the Hidden Past*. Mechanicsburg, PA: Stackpole Books, 2007.

Thornbury Farm Market & CSA. "History." Accessed December 2023. https://thornburyfarmcsa.com/history/.

Twaddell, Meg. *Inns, Tales and Taverns of Chester County*. Country Publications, 1984.

Warden, Rosemary. "The Infamous Fitch: The Tory Bandit, James Fitzpatrick of Chester County." *Pennsylvania History* 62, no. 3 (July 1, 1995): 376–87. https://journals.psu.edu/phj/article/view/25246/25015.

Watson, William. *The Ghosts of Duffy's Cut: The Irish Who Died Building America's Most Dangerous Stretch of Railroad*. Westport, CT: Praeger, 2006.

Watson, William, and Francis Watson. *Massacre at Duffy's Cut: Tragedy & Conspiracy on the Pennsylvania Railroad*. Charleston, SC: History Press, 2018.

"Who Was Sandy Flash?" MidAtlantic Roots. Accessed December 2023. https://midatlanticroots.com/drupal/chester-county/who-was-sandy-flash/.

Wilson, Patty. *The Pennsylvania Ghost Guide, Vol. I*. Roaring Spring, PA: Piney Creek, 2000.

"The Witch House of Exton . . . a/k/a What Was the Whelen/Ferrell/Meredith Farm." Chester County Ramblings. Last modified April 20, 2018. https://chestercountyramblings.com/2018/04/20/the-witch-house-of-exton-a-k-a-what-was-the-whelen-ferrell-meredith-farm/.

# About the Author

Kevin Lagowski is a public affairs and communications specialist. He previously worked for over a decade in broadcast television following his education in communications and film studies. Kevin has enjoyed the spooky and the supernatural since he was a child and would write "books" for his parents and stage "haunted houses" in the basement. He and his family now take regular day trips to see odd and offbeat sites. He spends the rest of his free time as a sports enthusiast / freelance writer, and his work can be found on sites such as thatballsouttahere.com and broadstreetbuzz.com, as well as his personal site, phillysportscomplex.com. He resides in Lincoln University, Pennsylvania with his wife, two sons, and good dog, Lexi.